FASHION ME A PEOPLE

FASHION ME A PEOPLE

Man, Woman, and the Church

by Eugene C. Kennedy, M.M.

SHEED AND WARD: NEW YORK

© *Sheed and Ward, Inc., 1967*

Library of Congress Catalog Card Number 67-21914

Nihil Obstat:
  Rev. Leo J. Steady, Ph.D., S.T.D.

Imprimatur:
  † Robert F. Joyce
  Bishop of Burlington
  July 11, 1967

The Nihil Obstat and Imprimatur are official declarations that a book or pamphlet is considered to be free of doctrinal or moral error. No implication is contained therein that those who have granted this Nihil Obstat or Imprimatur agree with the contents, opinions or statements expressed.

Manufactured in the United States of America

Contents

Introduction

IN the rainy April week in which I write these words the Catholic Church is the message in every medium. Several years ago the Church broke out of the back pages of religious news, those finely veined gray acres of news print, broken by occasional pictures of startled looking canons or Sunday soloists. Ever since Pope John opened the shutters of the Church, the world has taken to looking through our windows. It has found such a lively panorama of intertwined personalities and policies that it will never allow the Church to do its business in private again. The front pages and the television screens fairly teem with news about the Church, mostly concerning the agonies and conflicts of postconciliar renewal.

It is true that journalists revel in finding ecclesiastical heroes and villains for their pieces. They constantly misunderstand and oversimplify as they search the available facts for what will make the best story. Nevertheless, the attention of the world's press is a sign of the times and we cannot fail to understand it. The efforts of the Church to renew itself constitute one of the major news events of this decade. It is history in the making. Its eager chroniclers sense, at least dimly, the immense implications of a venerable religious body's attempts to relate itself more effectively to the world. Isn't that religion's real business, they ask, perhaps at the edges of their own consciousness, as they record the daily developments of the postconciliar era. The world is interested in the Church because the Church has restated its interest in the world.

Beyond this, the Church has discovered that part of being relevant is to take the risk of doing business in the open. Klieg lights, press conferences, and shouldering and shouting reporters have provided a new and intensely demanding environment for Church spokesmen. The free press, for all its faults, does not allow individuals or institutions whose concern is mankind to operate behind closed doors. This has been an unnerving experience for ecclesiastics who have not been accustomed to explaining themselves or their decisions. The Church which has preached truth and justice as great human values is constantly reminded of its obligations to display these in its practice. So in the week in which I write a theology professor at a great Catholic University has become a prominent news figure because the world demands that what we do in secret be brought into the light. The Pope has made the headlines for seeking peace not only between nations, but also between two of his own Cardinals. Catholic teachers strike in Chicago, laymen claim to be an integral part of the Church and organize themselves to prove it: these are just a sampling of the front page stories of the last few days.

This focus of the news media is fortunate because it does not allow us to forget our commitment to the truth in all our dealings with men. It is also a great glaring sign of the Church whose accidental forms are evolving on the great spotlighted stage of the world itself. The Church can no longer use the backdrop of turreted and bannered medieval pageantry and practice. The secret styles of outdated European Church politics are not now good enough to satisfy men who want to know more about this Church that proclaims salvation to them. The Church is indeed changing and, while this does not affect its essential nature as the extension of Christ's Incarnation, it demands a new order of things in many areas.

The Church has defined itself as a People on pilgrimage, and the process of revealing itself in this deeply human way is now under way. The world is witness to our struggles and, even though it may misunderstand and misreport them at times, it will not allow us to forget that we are present, according to our own claims, for the sake of all men. We cannot exist or renew just for ourselves. The heavy historical insulation of previous ages has worn through and we do not live in our own world anymore. That is what the headlines, the hustling journalists, and their eager readers are telling us.

The danger would be to misinterpret the attention we receive as merely that of gossips and mindless critics. The danger is increased by all those who fail to understand that the Church must urgently open itself to a refashioning of its forms of relationship to the world. The hour is already late to embrace the task of renewal with something more than minor modifications in mind.

If the accidental forms of the Church are some Joseph's coat, there is lots of cleaning and repair work to be done. The thread of vocational supply, for example, has been given a sharp tug, and the whole garment seems to be unravelling. The development of new forms for all the Church's apostolates cannot be delayed. God will not blindly provide for a basically improvident people.

It is to the questions connected with understanding the

Church as a People and the development of forms to express this reality adequately that these pages are addressed.

If the Church is a people, then it is man and woman, and the institutions of the Church must develop themselves in accord with the healthy fullness of human personality. The essays of which this book is composed represent my own reflections on the human issues involved in the process of renewal. I do not offer them as definitive but as sources of stimulation. Nobody understands all the issues involved in aggiornamento. I have had the opportunity over the past several years to be close to the personal dimension of the struggle of Churchmen and Churchwomen to understand themselves and their work for the redemption of the world. What I offer in these pages arises from my contact with sincere and generous people who love the Church deeply and who wish to give themselves to it completely. This book centers on themes concerning the human expression of the Church. This is not to display or criticize the flaws that anything human possesses, but to point out the great potential of the human person, under the guidance of the Spirit, for fuller growth.

This book is, in a sense, about the spiritual life. I have only recently sensed the utter simplicity of this concept. I believe that the spiritual life has for too long suffered, like modern education, from jargonese. Endless commentaries have staked out the geography of the spiritual life, its ways and byways, its laws and bylaws. The emphasis has been so much on the *practice* of the spiritual life, that the notion of its being a *life* has been somewhat obscured. Quite simply, however, the spiritual life is the life of the Spirit. Geographically-minded people may chart their individual journeys, but their insistence on drawing handy maps for everyone has not been an altogether successful enterprise. The human person, especially through his relationship with other persons, must find his own way in response to the promptings of the Spirit. The Church speaks the words of eternal life not to tightly formed regiments but to free men and women. Full manhood and womanhood is indispensable to the members of the Church called to be a people together for the sake of all men. I feel deeply that we must bring all our genius and creativity to the development of institutions which will allow men and women to find themselves fully so that they may give themselves fully in their servant vocations. The environment for true growth in the life of the Spirit is freedom. The Church must provide forms that are human and flexible enough to allow the mystery of growth in grace to take place. Older ways, based on a lesser understanding of man, are no longer serviceable. This affects the lives of all the Church's pilgrim peoples: priests, religious, and laity.

I have not provided blueprints for these forms and so must deliberately disappoint or frustrate those who will fault me for not having done so. I have discussed, with an admittedly limited vision, the realities that must be understood as we seek together the forms that will take us, as the People of God, into the future. It would be presumptuous to provide detailed plans right now. I do not think that we have the solid evidence of experimentation or the wisdom to provide these answers as yet. We can, however, understand the direction of our journey better if we understand man and woman better. It is in understanding them in the depth of their relationship with each other that we grasp the meaning of the Church itself.

It is my hope that these reflections will be a small contribution to the task of renewal that is a genuine response to the action of the Spirit. That response must be a free one, achieved openly and at the price of making mistakes. We can thank God that the world will not allow us the luxury of speculating on these problems in secret. Some will find a few of my thoughts disturbing. I hope they are not too disturbed, but I certainly hope they are disturbed. We can all too easily end up on the back pages again, right next to the obituaries.

It has been a great blessing to have shared the struggles of earnest Catholics on all levels. I have been privileged to be associated with bishops and superiors as well as priests, religious, and laymen on the front lines of the Church's work for renewal. In a sense I am asking you not to listen to my voice but to the voices I have listened to. They belong to sincere and forthright Christians who are not trying to save themselves and who gladly risk themselves in trying to save others. The fortunes of assignment have brought me to live for the last several years in the middle of America, a well-recognized locus of vigorous and determined experimentation. No greater experience could have been granted me than to have worked closely with the priests, religious, and lay people of Chicago. Particularly inspiring has been the opportunity to share in the development of the Association of Chicago Priests, that group of men determined to serve the Church through their ordinary as fully as possible. It has been a singular blessing to have superiors like Father John McCormack, the Superior General of Maryknoll, who has allowed me complete freedom to make my own mistakes in speaking and writing.

An author has many debts to his friends that he can never repay, even by mentioning them in an introduction. I am grateful to the Maryknoll Fathers and the Maryknoll Sisters throughout the world. Of those whose frequent contact has meant much to me, I must mention Father Thomas Peyton, M.M., a priest who does live by the Spirit. Father Andrew Greeley may be best known as a priest-sociologist but I know him as a close friend and helpful critic. In this year of his fiftieth birthday, I must mention Dan Herr, who never stops pushing his friends to do better and more constructive work. To these, and the many unmentioned, I am deeply grateful.

Eugene C. Kennedy, m.m.

Glen Ellyn, Illinois
April 22, 1967
   F.S.

FASHION ME A PEOPLE

I/THE CHURCH AS A PERSON

1 / The Silent Schism

"LUTHER," according to Tillmans, "was born in the Middle Ages and died in modern times." At Luther's birth the great stage settings of history were being shifted into place for the enactment of the drama of the sixteenth century. A new world was to be discovered; Selim the Grim was to march across the map to the gates of Vienna; humanism was to flower; and the Church, lurching like the slow-motion pictures of a cathedral in the grip of an earthquake, was to shudder apart.

The parallels for our time can admittedly be exaggerated or inexact. Twentieth-century man does, however, stand at the edge of a new age of exploration and discovery. The human race is just on the near side of a new world and a new way of life. In the midst of these stirrings, the Church finds itself, in many of its accidental forms at least, tumbling apart once more.

The great confusion for the Church at this time does not arise from inner corruption. The great heaving and buckling of the Church's structure is a result of the massive effort at reorienting itself in the modern world. This is implicit in the Church's redefinition of itself as the People of God. It finds itself absorbed and inextricably caught up in the world that is its environment. Previous forms of relationship to the world, such as the model of the walled city that supported separation from all that was secular, are now magnificent ruins. They are no longer accepted as realistic, either theologically, psychologically, or sociologically.

Progress is always managed badly. What we look back on as great periods of transition or development were, in reality, generations of incredible pain and suffering for the people caught up in them. Historical processes are relentless and unforgiving. Because it brought us into the modern world, it is easy to forget the human price of something like the Industrial Revolution. Forgotten are the hundreds of thousands of families who had to survive without hope and were crushed by this process of adjustment.

So it was during the Protestant revolt and the Catholic reformation. So it is today. In the sixteenth and other centuries that found us more sure of ourselves, we were able to define our problems in terms such as "heresy" and "schism." These concepts caught the distortions of doctrine and made them, as the adversaries of truth, somewhat easier to deal with. The enemy is always better when clearly identifiable.

The Church is presently experiencing the stresses of reorganizing and reordering itself in the world of men. These are as intense as any experienced in other ages of adjustment. The clefts in belief and behavior observable within the overall Christian community would, in another time, have been labeled in some approximate fashion as "schism" or "heresy." The reality underlying those terms exists across the Church today. We just lack a good name for it and so we call it by no name at all. We may have good reasons to avoid christening it and thus polarizing divergent views even further. It is nonetheless there, a silent schism, the reflection of the fragmented and developing state of the Church at this time. The elements of this are not deliberately malicious or divisive. Nobody planned it this way. It is just that, as the clouds of dust settle a bit, we find Christians in conflict and in doubt in many areas and they question rather than receive comfort from the teaching authority of the Church.

The People of God are on pilgrimage, but it is a journey full of pondering. The desert of our wandering is hot and dry and all the horizons are distant. We will consider some of the signs of silent schism in the following pages.

THE MEANING OF THE CHURCH

There is an undeniable communications gap between the Church as teacher and the Church as people. The rich understandings of the Church that were quite remarkably achieved in the brief years of the Vatican Council II have only slowly been filtering down to all the members of the Church. Christian reeducation is obviously an exhausting and extremely difficult task. Perhaps in earlier eras the conditions of culture allowed this to occur gradually. Modern man no longer has such leisure for learning. He cannot survive without immediate and massive information from teachers whom he can trust. The modern Catholic, clerical or lay, except in unusual circumstances, has experienced the end products of conciliar change (as in liturgical reform) in a very personal way, but without sufficient preparation or understanding for them. The changes, however, have often been perceived by those experiencing them as disruptive and upsetting. There has been a failure of Christian preaching to illumine renewed Christian practice. The leaders of the Church have been perceived as assenting in the conciliar documents to truths that many of them seemingly did not understand. There are refurbished truths and hopeful promises, but there is a frustrating delay in the implementation of these. Granting the difficulties involved in carrying out the tasks of education and progress intelligently, the result of not doing these effectively has created an unsettled environment throughout the Church.

Christians everywhere are unsure of the Church and its leaders who had previously provided such serene and self-assured guidance. Men are wondering, in the communications gap that threatens to be one of credibility as well, what in reality they do or do not believe. Many emblems of Catholic practice, incidental though they may always have been, are suddenly gone, but gone with them is the quality of psychological cohesiveness they had previously guaranteed. Men feel shorn of the basic elements of vigorous faith, such as fasting, and they have not been helped sufficiently to understand why. Men and women who accepted the Church's teaching on birth control at great personal sacrifice suddenly find that after all their suffering, they may have been misinformed after all. Priests and religious who gave unquestioning assent to whatever tasks and obligations the Church pointed out as sanctifying suddenly find that they may have been misled. A blind faith in the Church's leaders and teachers has yielded to a terrifying doubt for Catholics that they should ever have been so willing to surrender their lives to a framework that is now openly being abandoned.

These Catholics find themselves somewhat dazed and bewildered and unable to forgive themselves for what they feel was a naive and culpable innocence about the real facts of life. They feel that they paid the price of belief and accepted all that this seemed to demand. They built their lives on theories that are being questioned or repudiated and they feel betrayed. They are in a stressful situation because an adequate theological formation that really speaks to their needs has not yet been provided. What are they to believe or to trust in now of this teaching authority that has seemed to fail them? They are by no means sure. Therefore, many have struck out, in understandable efforts to establish a Gospel-based stability in their lives, in a variety of directions.

THE CLERGY

Priests throughout the world have felt the moorings of their lives cut. In the consequent confusion it seems frequently as though it were every man for himself. They feel as put upon as the layman has felt for years in a Church where, despite the Vatican II documents, they feel something like forgotten men. Allowing for the fact that this provides a great opportunity for growth, many of the clergy feel increasingly restive within ecclesiastical structures which in fact give them little chance to grow. The paternalistic approach of many bishops that worked so well in the past does not reassure but antagonizes priests in the present. It may well be that the priesthood in general is passing through an adolescent phase of growth. No longer the obedient and dutiful child, the priest senses his individuality and potential personal worth. It should not surprise us to see him engaged in a struggle for a better relationship with the authority figures in his life. They have turned out, as parents do for teenagers, to be mortals rather than gods. A readjustment to this reality is underway.

The priesthood is quite clearly in the throes of growth toward more independent and responsible manhood. There is probably something appropriate, in this developing stage, about his thinking about getting married and living a life that is more truly his own. This is the vision of manhood passed on to all men in a free environment and it is rapidly becoming the ideal of clergymen who no longer intend to serve with anything less than their full manhood. Tragic for the Church is the reduction of this struggle for growth in priests and religious to some simplistic problem of authority challenged by the disobedient.

In general, however, authority has not recognized the dynamics of the uneasiness in the ranks of the clergy and religious. The clergy are reacting, in the spirit of theologically guaranteed personal freedom, against what they perceive as a distant authoritarianism in ecclesiastical structure. Too many superiors react in turn to this reaction rather than to the roots of the entire situation. They try to stem the tide pressing for a collegial sharing of the apostolate. This is often under a sense of threat from these basically healthy manifestations. The rift between superior and subjects is widened and the conflict truly deepened.

Were there a greater degree of communication between ordinaries and priests, a greater willingness to make collegiality concrete, the phenomenon of multiplying associations of priests would not have occurred. These associations are telling us something about what is happening in the Church if we would try to listen and understand. The clergy are forging groups, not all of which fit under Canon Law, that represent power in dialogue with the authority of the ordinary. Priests are saying through these movements that they cannot live on promises and deferred aggiornamento. They feel that the Church is not the exclusive possession of any one group in it and they intend to express their convictions and ideals as clearly as possible. They assert their own need to be regarded and respected as men. The first position paper voted in by the 1300 member Association of Chicago Priests was tellingly entitled "Priesthood and Manhood."

These groups of priests are not disobedient or disloyal. They express a great willingness to respond to the needs of the Church through their ordinary. They are saying, however, that a new relationship must be acknowledged and developed in the apostolate. They represent a new force, unpredictable and perhaps unthinkable ten years ago, in the composition of the Church. Where the ordinary or superior tries to contain rather than cooperate with these movements, tension is increased. These forces can never be shunted aside or ignored. It is not business in the same old way anymore, and a general acknowledgment of this fact cannot safely be delayed much longer.

These same priests find deep questions of personal and professional identity proposed to them. The image of the priest has shifted radically in the public press and entertainment from that of the man of good-natured peace to the man of unresolved conflict. The Christianity they counted on has turned out to be culturally conditioned to a surprising degree. For all the years of preaching and teaching Catholics have apparently not been convinced at a deep level on major human questions such as racial justice.

The clergy and religious of Chicago could only search their hearts in view of their clear rejection by the Catholic suburbanites who have chosen to defend their property rights rather than encourage open housing. These lay people, who have supported and sustained the Church through good years and bad, are not pleased with clergymen who march through their neighborhoods to protest their all-white character. Something has been missing in the sharing of the message of Christ in dioceses where the unity of priests and people has turned out to be a fragile and easily destroyed entity. Serious Catholics at all levels have had to contemplate the possibility that what they have provided was veneer rather than substance in Christian conviction. These tensions are real and have alienated priests and people in many areas. Are these hardworking people who prize their families and their property to be condemned for choosing these rather than deeper Christian values to live by?

THE LAITY

So too, a better educated laity feels the same desire to share in the responsibility of the People of God. A new generation, inspirited by Vatican II, seeks to give itself and its energies to the Church, but these laymen are frustrated at the lack of viable structures to make this a reality. In many places they have chosen to live out their convictions quite apart from the traditional framework of parish life. They feel undernourished by the preaching they hear and unconvinced about many of the apostolic aims of the dioceses in which they find themselves. They resent not being consulted about building programs and fund-raising drives that they must finance. In great sincerity they speculate about the future of Catholic school systems that have been questioned on many grounds. Does the Catholic population of the United States wish to insulate itself from American society? Are the fears that only through Catholic schools and consequent Catholic subcultures can their faith be preserved really justified? They wonder, as vocations to the priesthood and religious life diminish, who will staff these schools in another generation. They agonize over whether their faith can only be sustained by expensive extensions of separatism from their own culture. These questions are hard but honest ones. The laity feel that these must be answered before they can assent to pay the bills for American Catholic education.

In large numbers these younger generation Catholics are

forging their own personal answers. They do not at all reject the Gospel and the essential meaning of the Church but they are already departing markedly from the practice of the faith as it was preserved by their parents. Many make moves on their own to express their faith in a way that no longer fits the context of traditional parochial life. The widespread response to "underground" parishes, to worship in homes rather than churches, to a Christianity that is in some sense extra-territorial, are facts. Nobody can confront these without speculating on their implications for a vigorous and healthy institutional Church. This schism, if it can be so termed, becomes less silent every day.

RELIGIOUS

The religious are as restive as the diocesan clergy and the laity. There has been an observable lack of confidence in traditional forms of dedicated service to the People of God. The healthiest and most creative religious are seriously debating whether the staples of convent and monastery life are any longer appropriate. It is true that many eccentric and ill-balanced religious have been part of the negative reaction to structures they dislike. The tremors that run through the world of the professed religious do not, however, find their entire explanation in this and cannot be dismissed in any summary fashion.

Deep questions about the size, purpose, and styles of life of religious groups are being posed by the most sincere and dedicated members of these communities. They are struggling against the forces that desperately hope everything will fall neatly back into preconciliar place again. Experimental communities have only begun to emerge as the first signs of human persons who want to give their lives in a whole-

hearted way to the People of God. Underlying these moves is
the conviction that Christianity is not a ritualistic framework
lived by rote and that something more human must be possible in view of the theology of Vatican II. These people are
willing to embrace poverty, chastity, and obedience, but they
are newly sensitive to their birthrights as human persons and
they are not ready to cashier these unconsciously anymore.
They do not believe anymore that the resurrected life of the
Spirit finds its ultimate expression in infinitely codified lives.

It is quite impossible for the Church to move backward
and to leave these phenomena unacknowledged. The silent
schism only flourishes when the Church, through its institutions and leaders, fails to come to terms with the realities of
Catholic life in the last part of the twentieth century. There
is no doubt that a healthy and life-giving response can be
given by the Church to all the stirrings of growth within it.
Each day, however, intensifies these problems. They must
be attended to with great patience, understanding, and a
mature acknowledgment of the Church as the People of God.
But they must be attended to or the present structures of
the institutional Church will only disintegrate at an ever
accelerating rate. The great task is to begin to think out and
bring into being the structures that will carry the Church
into the twenty-first century.

THE TIME IS NOW

There is surely nothing easier than to complain and be con-
temptuous about ecclesiastical forms that have served out
their useful days. It is the cynic's solution, however, to revel
in the rubble of what he has destroyed. Far more difficult is
the task of facing the Church with deep reverence and respect
for it as the vast trembling assemblage of Christians making

its way through history. Infinitely more trying to those who love the Church is to think out the alternative expressions of Christian life and belief that will contain the People of God on their pilgrimage into the future.

"Game-Theory," used by social scientists and others, suggests that, when there is time, it is better to think and plan rather than not to do so. It is to reflect on the nature of the Church as a mystery of persons in relationship to one another and to speculate on the basic convictions that must give rise to future apostolic forms that these chapters are directed. This book does not offer *the* master plan. It is an attempt to understand the men and women who are the Church and to provide adequate human directions for the expression of the Church's mission. It is written with the conviction that there is indeed time to think and plan, rather than wail and despair. The Spirit is available whenever we are open to it, and the time of salvation is now.

2/Man, Woman, and the Church

MORE often than not in the finely turned fictions of John O'Hara man and woman meet and destroy each other through their relationships. These interpersonal disasters, documented with the details of all the days O'Hara has lived through, reveal the other side of the Christian possibilities of life. But there could be no tales of despair and longing at all if human relationships were not capable of hope and fullness.

These stories are printed in ink blended from the bitter residue of lives all gone wrong. But in a curious, failed way, they reveal the rich potential of what men and women can do for each other. Even O'Hara's men and women search in a blunted and unrelieved way for the completeness of themselves through sharing with each other. It is because they stop short at selfish grabbing that the rewards of real love lie always beyond them.

"Life is the right place for love," Robert Frost wrote, "I don't know where it's likely to go better." And the richest expression and source of love arises in the relationship of man and woman. The history of the race and of too many individuals tells us how this relationship can fail. Yet the life stages of each person show that growth leads through an

evolving series of relationships that are crowned by readiness
to meet maturely with and to grow in relationship to the
opposite sex. From the state of being loved, of being fed
emotionally by others, man must pass to the state of loving,
of nourishing the other freely and fully. From the chum-stage,
the like-sexed pairs and groups of the childhood years, the
individual moves inevitably toward the challenge of a mature
heterosexual relationship. This transcends the physical capa-
bility of sexual performance as the sunrise does the spark. It
demands a total relationship in which genital sexuality is
integrated in the person. Because it is marked with real love,
it brings forth the fullness of the man and the woman. It
gives them life, but demands constant growth in the cadences
of their giving and receiving together through the years. In
the context of their relationship they are able to bring new
lives, healthy and full of hope, into the same cycle of growth
that has been theirs. Life for those in love is not a sweetened
sail toward a sunny horizon. There are lashing storms, the
perils of every human passage, and this man-woman relationship must develop or it is quickly done in. But the
growth pivots always on the total relationship of the partners
with each other, on their thorough sharing of self and life
together.

In marriage, the strength of this relationship depends on
whether it is between a full man and woman who are un-
mistakably husband and wife to each other. The validity of
this will markedly affect the possibilities of growth for their
children. If the relationship is faulted in a major way, the
children are cruelly fated to personal problems. These difficulties often manifest themselves in the children's inability
to identify themselves in a healthy way as male or female. The
research on homosexuality, for example, which is still admittedly fragmentary, relates the presence of homosexuality

in the boy to a weak and ineffective father. Nobody is an
ineffective father who has not been an ineffective husband first. Something flawed in the manhood of the
father fouls the delicate interpersonal dynamics that go
into the making of his sons. If the relationship of the husband and wife is distorted, the children lack the models of
identification they need for a healthy integration of the elements of their own personhood.

It is true as well that, in some cases at least, the healing
of these invisible wounds is accomplished only through a
healthy personal relationship later in life. In these later relationships the love and acceptance of the partner enable the
person to grow again. The best predictor for a happy marriage
still remains the happiness of the marriage of the parents of
the prospective bride and groom. Disorder in the most demanding male-female relationship does indeed breed death,
just as health and love in this relationship give rise to life.

The world has come only lately to a genuine appreciation
of mutuality between the sexes. The Church has also only
gradually understood that the summit of human relationships, that between man and woman, is never reached on the
unbalanced pathways of exclusive male dominance. That man
and woman are equal human persons, whose mystery of sharing
is at the heart of understanding life, has not always been its
prime philosophical or theological teaching. The Church, it
could be said, is, in company with the rest of the world, just
beginning to understand the human person. If there has been
an acknowledged development and deepening of theological
knowledge through the centuries, there has been the same kind
of development in comprehending man in the human condition. Gone, thankfully, are the days when it was felt that
women were males who, because a south wind was blowing
or the seed was weak, did not quite make it. The battle of

the sexes is not over, but the imperious banners of masculine superiority have been shredded badly and some have fallen into the dust. We have begun to see that the story of mankind centers on man and woman as equal sharers in humanity. Perhaps it is not too much to say that whether this story will have a happy ending depends very much on whether the goals of full manhood and full womanhood are realized in this world. These goals are unattainable by the sexes separated from one another.

If humanity is to have fullness, it comes only through the growth of men and women in concrete relationship to one another. If the Church is the People of God, and not an army or a barnacled bureaucracy, then it grows only through its human elements. Organizational charts and finely webbed hierarchical structures fail for the Church when their roots are in political power instead of personal growth. The People of God will reach its fullness, not as a triumphant conquering army, but in the richness of men and women growing together in the life of the Spirit. Love has never been successful as a cold abstraction, although large icy chunks of it clog the rivers of Catholic thought. Love is the vital sign of people sharing life generously together. And if we are ever to bring mature love into the world, it will grow in its only possible environment, the men and women who, as the People of God, are open to a full share of life together.

God's action in this world is always accommodated to the human condition. The only forces that can frustrate the action of the Spirit are the scabrous defenses that men clutch at to protect their self-esteem. Selfish men, men whose goal is to save only their own skins or reputations, are undeveloped in all of life's relationships. They are defended against finding and knowing themselves and are, therefore, incapable of opening any real self to another. They may squirm under their burden of loneliness, they may inhabit the soulless chapters of an O'Hara novel that open on one another like a succession of empty rooms, but they never attain real love by grabbing for it. The Spirit of love operates in them only when they have yielded the inner defenses that shut them off from the only source of life. This is the "old man" who must die before the "new man" can come to life from within.

The whole context of the resurrected Christian life centers on the surrender of ourselves to the Spirit sent to abide with and to enliven us. This action of God matches the way man is made. It functions in harmony with the authentic dimensions of humanity. If life and love are transmitted not through plans, pleas, or pageantry but through personal relationships, then this is how the Spirit "acts" in the world. The New Pentecost, much like the first, reaches institutions through individuals in relationship to one another. The fullest action of the Spirit can be expected where there is the fullest experience of humanity, where defenses have been put aside, where people reveal their true selves as the sole genuine basis of human giving and receiving. This simple thesis of God's action being sensitively attuned to the quality of personal sharing suggests that his fullest manifestation will take place in the context of those human relationships that have the richest potential. This bounty of possibilities is built into the relationship between man and woman, the elements that sum up humanity itself.

God's work in the world depends, then, on our full realization of the manhood and womanhood of the People of God in relationship to one another. This is the inevitable conclusion to our recent recognition of the equal share men and women have in humanity. That is why it makes little sense to speak of granting rights to women, or finding a place for them in the Church, as though it were basically a generously disposed masculine enterprise. For too long we have tried to make individuals fit into preconceived and culturally derived institutional models of the Church. We have cast these aside now in favor of the glimpse of the true meaning of the Church we get by describing it as the mystery of the People of God. There is no stopping at this point to rest content with a more comfortable and flexible ecclesial concept. Logic leads us on to examine and understand the human nature of these people, the conditions in which they grow, the panorama of realities that emerges from facing the full humanity in which the saving mystery is set. This cannot be accomplished by thinking about men but only by meeting them in the human condition.

Without this confrontation with the nature of the persons who are the People of God, no understanding of the Church itself is possible. It will always be glimpsed from the outside, with the impersonal measurements inherited from institutional models that are no longer appropriate. The Church is even now ceding the monarchical self-concept which it almost unconsciously assumed as it made its way through history. It clothed itself in a regal culture that was dissolved in most earthly kingdoms.

The funeral of King Edward VII, in the heart of what some people persist in calling the "good years," was the last gathering of the crowned and coroneted heads of European grandeur in its death throes. The plumes and finery of this last of princely processions bobbed in the sun not because of the cobbled London streets or uneasy horses but because the world itself was already shuddering underfoot. It was the final public performance for the traditions of empires built on the divine right of kings and the virtual slavery of their subjects. Within a few years those incredible cousins, the king, the kaiser, and the tsar, saw the end of the age of empire. A new era of governments based on at least some recognition of the rights and hopes of individual people came into being.

The present transformation of the structures of the Church is the sign of the same thing happening just fifty years later. The questioning of princes of privilege, courtly trappings, the quiet and uncomplaining service of the lesser members to the support and sustenance of the monarchical model are symbols of a Church shaken by the same tremor that ran through the world half a century ago. The essential Church is not threatened by this splintering of a system that was historically and culturally accidental. Threat arises only if churchmen do not realize that this is in fact occurring. But the sign of the postconciliar times underscores personal freedom and points to a decentralization of power. Emphasis has been placed on a collegial concept of authority as service to the People of God, themselves a community of loving persons.

In effect, the first steps have been taken in the process of the Church's gigantic and painful journey toward relationship to men as they are. The turmoil and tension of this transformation are very great, so great in fact that some back away and many miss the meaning of what is happening. Some long for a restoration of the past as did the exiled royalty of the twenties. Others prophesy a structureless era, even as anarchy was an ideal for the revolutionists of the world as the twentieth century was born. The task, however, is to develop new and healthy structures that will allow the Church to place itself properly at the service of the human family.

These structures will not emerge through the destruction of all authority and law any more than they could emerge out of a decaying monarchical model. The new structures must meet the nature and needs of the persons who constitute the

People of God. The Spirit is operating, in this personalistic age, through individuals in open and loving relationships. These in turn will inform the institutions for the new era. If the Church is to find itself, it will be because these persons, men and women, have first found the fullness of themselves. One can agree without discouragement that even these new structures will be imperfect and in need of constant growth and development. One can assent to this because it is part of what it means for the People of God to move through history subject to all the forces that condition the form of its journey in any age. The Church's passage into new and more human structures will not be accomplished easily, but it will be accomplished successfully if its foundations arise from an ever deeper acknowledgement and embrace of humanity itself. The Church's role remains to make itself incarnate, to take on the flesh and blood of humankind. The fullest realization of this mission comes from a recognition that authentic life arises only out of concrete loving relationships. In these days of footless slogans, many yearn to be "where the action is." The true environment for the Church, however, is to be "where life is lived," the landscape of the living.

We have been hung up on the symbols of the past, some of them even scriptural, in our efforts to apportion the apostolate. Too often we have tried to make the Bible or other sources fit into our preconceptions about the human race. We have justified slavery, among other things, in times when we were not so sure that all men should be free. Worse still, we have perpetuated an imbalance in the relationship of the People of God by reinforcing the masculine element to the constant disadvantage of the feminine. The Scriptures have been read with the distorting spectacles of cultures that have felt that this must be so. We have failed, I suppose, to sense the utter humanity of the scripture writers themselves.

Largely because of the pressure of non-Catholic scholarship, we have begun to understand how completely these writers were men of their own culture, tracing their papyri with the images and symbols of their own times.

How crowded with human cries the Bible seems! And how simply and quickly the earthy realists of an earlier era used sexual metaphors to describe the relationship of God and his people. They were not offering a model of the relationship that should obtain between the sexes for all time as much as they were employing the deepest symbols of human sharing that they had at hand. Do you want to know how much God loves Israel, they ask; what his relationship to his people is like? A lover who always forgives, the faithful, full-hearted husband awaiting his bride. Nothing came more naturally to the minds of men who wanted to express, in the only language they had, something about the relationship between God and his chosen ones.

We have hung many a priori ideas about men and women on these phrases. Somewhere along the way we forgot that these were anguished words wrung out of burning hearts bent on saying something about God, not something undying about the men and women who are his people. Their message was that there can be no flicker of understanding God's faithfulness if we do not understand something about the intensity for sharing life that lovers know.

The way is still the same. We might see that the kind of relationships we have with each other still give some reflection of God's love for the world. The love that should characterize his people is not something they just think about. It is what they live through with each other; it is the source of their community, the reality of relationship that they celebrate in their liturgy. This can be a sacrament of sharing only when it arises from the richest and most relevant of human relationships, that of man and woman. When we have plumbed the dimensions of this relationship, we will have understood the People of God, not as we might presume or wish them to be, but as they are. The viable institutional structures of the future will prove secure and be a source of service to the world when they are built on this realistic understanding of man and his ways in this world.

Our understanding of the Church of men and women is important for marriage, of course, but it has implications for all levels of its activity. The evolution of the expression of the priesthood and religious life in the renewed Church must flow from the same informed understanding. The Canon Law of the Church, meant to encompass the activity of its people in a healthy way, will have a soul only if it meets the realities of humanity. The Church as the extension of the Incarnation can enflesh itself as the mystery of love only when it is able to allow the Spirit to speak through the human beings who are God's people. Hope for the ages to come arises from our faith in the full possibilities of human beings who are in open relationships to each other. Relevance to the human race is the inevitable consequence of mature relevance to one another.

We may indeed sing the praise of friendship to extol its presence among men or among women. This is part of real life, but it is not the whole of it. Rich and strengthening as these relationships are between members of the same sex within the Church, they can never be the highest source of growth for it. It is, naturally, safer, in a sense, to confine our speculations about the possibilities of human relationships to these categories, especially when we speak of the priesthood and religious life. But we have a small measure of faith and a diminished sense of humanity, if we think this kind of separatism can be successful enough for the needs of the Church and the world in the future.

The mystery of the growth of the human race into a community depends on the healthy interaction throughout the Church of its masculine and feminine elements. This is not furthered by theory but by developing the conditions in which the relationships of God's flesh and blood servants can work in healthy and mature ways together. The future of the Church, about which so many wonder and others despair, will be found in its reaffirmation of its male-female composition. Otherwise, the voices which charge that the Church preaches love and practices something else will not be stilled but will grow louder. The Church, on the verge of full growth, will slip back to a tormented adolescence. The mystery of the Church is met only in man and woman in relationship to each other as the People of God.

3/The Dimensions of Humanity

ONLY a man who had a large view of life, its contradictions as well as its promises, could say, as did Pope John XXIII, that he had called a council "so that man's sojourn on earth might be less sad." These words of weathered wisdom can be spoken or understood by those with a mature feeling for the human condition. This phrase acknowledges the dark side of man's history but does not allow cynical surrender to it. These words are uttered in hope that is not overidealized and unrealistic. While this sentence recognizes that there is no immunity from pain and struggle, it also affirms that man has within himself the promise of growth and accomplishment.

Maturity, not elderliness, marks Pope John's phrase. It is the magic blend of believing in man without denying his failures. This seems the mark of maturity in any area of living. Fully grown men can face and accept the complexities of themselves and of history without unnecessarily distorting them out of fear. The first characteristic of the mature personality, accordng to many observers, is its openness to all of its experience. The mature person does not need the absolute categories of black and white, good or bad, to interpret his experience of life. The sign of his maturity is the balance of his perspective, the painfully achieved perspective of the human scene that belongs to those who are fully alive. The grown-up man can view all that he is. It is possible for him to live with the fact that he is still learning, still growing, still in the process of personal development.

Mankind presents many faces to us. We cannot be selective about those to which we would give our attention. If we are to understand man, we must face him whole, just as he is. Our task bids us to uncover the truth about man. Otherwise we will run the risk of serving and trying to save a preconceived image wrought by our own fancy or our own needs.

A fundamental fact, rooted in the Jewish tradition and written into the Scriptures, is that the human person is one entity. The researches of psychosomatic medicine have buttressed our belief in man's complex unity. He is not merely mind any more than he is merely flesh. Neither is he a principle of intellect pitted against a crowding rush of emotional impulses. Cartesian dualism despoiled man of the wealth of his oneness. Through the ages many theories, pragmatic and even ascetic, have been built on this riven model of man. They have led to tortured extremes of exaggerated spiritualism and materialism. It would be difficult to overestimate the amount of human suffering inflicted by these earnest pursuers of the Cartesian heritage. They have tried, with resultant pain for all concerned, to force man into a model for which he was not made.

The truth about man, confirmed by a renewed understanding of the Scriptures as well as the new understandings of psychology, is that he is an almost infinitely subtle unity. He is body and soul, intellect and emotions, all together and at the same time. The mutual influence of the elements of his being, as amplified by psychosomatic medicine, attest to the thoroughgoing unitary quality of his personhood. The aspects of his human existence may be separable and even antagonistic in intellectual analysis, but they are at home together in practice. Man, the culmination of creation, balances and blends the features of his humanity in the wholeness of his person.

One of the most intriguing things about mankind is this characteristic of balance as the basis of healthy life. Homeostasis is the name we give to the individual's self-adjusting balance of the biochemical elements in his makeup. Psychological measures point to the balance of masculine and feminine elements that go into the healthy fullness of manhood or womanhood. Sexual identification is not something limited to the procreative possibilities or responsibilities of any individual. It refers, in a broader way, to the total integration of the human qualities that go into the making of a man or a woman.

There is hardly need here to recapitulate or to try to settle the various theoretical approaches to the question of masculine and feminine differences. The eternal feminists and the environmentalists, each with their own reasons and their own evidence, have pressed for a recognition of the absolute differences or the basic similarities of man and woman. The real answer to this difference of opinion will come only when we let the fullness of human nature emerge in all those who possess it.

We can, however, reflect on the presence of what have been termed masculine and feminine elements within each individual. It is also possible to appreciate that a totally polarized understanding of human sexuality is a misunderstanding of human sexuality. To many minds, sexual identification as a real man or a real woman are points on the opposite ends of a long continuum of adjustment. At one

end are placed all the aggressive, intellectual qualities and
these are labeled male. At the opposite end are all the passive
and intuitive qualities. These are termed female. There is
great striving on the part of many uncertain individuals to
take on at least the outer behaviors appropriate to their sex.
To possess these qualities, or even this external show of them,
is very reassuring to the doubting masculine or feminine ego.

The question arises, midst the evidence that suggests that
much of man is a mixture, whether real men and women are
actually at clearly identifiable opposite end points on this
continuum. The experience of life and scientific research
suggest that this is not so.

The authentically healthy person represents a balance of
masculine and feminine elements. In each person the *animus,*
according to Jung, is echoed by the *anima.* The healthy man
is not at the extreme of crude masculinity. The healthy
woman is not at the opposite extreme of fainting femininity.
The fully developed individual integrates these broadly
sexual aspects of personality within himself. So the real man,
the real father for example, is not only strong, but also gentle.
He is not only a source of shelter and defense, but also of love
and affection for his family. He is strength but he is also
tenderness, and he is both at the same time. He is, we might
say, woman as well as man in his own fully realized personality. In the same way, the real woman is not only compassionate and caring, but sturdy and strong as well. She is
man as well as woman, with the best of humanity's possibilities in herself. The wholesome synthesis of the elements of
personality is health in any human being.

To admit that both man and woman share the common
elements of humanity is neither to deny their differences nor
falsely to dramatize them. This blend of qualities, the reflection of the androgynous nature of the human family, is

achieved by growth from within through a release of the potential for personal development of both sexes. To place full masculinity and full femininity at the opposite ends of a sexual continuum is to obscure the fact that the fullness of either can be achieved only in relationship to one another. This sole means of completion for each sex demands not distance from one another but open communication. This does not rule out a similarity in the man and woman's sharing of humanity, but neither does it proclaim that there is only one sex, somehow accidentally and incidentally culturally differentiated.

A more helpful model presents the ends of our previously imagined continuum or line bent up to form a circle. This places the stark, unyielding extremes of hardened masculinity and fragile femininity right next to each other as the line closes in a completed sphere. Both are caricatures of healthy adjustment and they are contiguous in the wasteland of personal disorder. Psychological bonds unite the men and women who adapt these poses to prove and protect themselves. Their personality dynamics are akin in this homeland of the homosexual, the sterile, isolated breeding ground of unhealthy life.

The healthy man and the healthy woman are to be found on exactly the opposite side of this circle. Here both sexes are unself-consciously sure of their adulthood. Here the man is as clearly masculine as the woman is feminine. However, neither of these states can be understood except as a splendid and proportioned sharing of the finest qualities of both. This sets the stage for the rich exchange that occurs in the relationship of man and woman.

The fullest possible life comes when there is a maximal disclosure of the self to the other. This leads to new life and to an ever deeper discovery and realization of the person of the man or woman in the relationship. The real man and the real woman find the fulfillment of their humanity, pursuing their individual stars and realizing their gifts, in ceding themselves to each other. There is a dying in the mature meeting of man and woman, but it is the prelude and precondition for life to the full for both of them. It is in this meeting of man and woman, each a healthy balance of personality elements, that the genuine fullness of human nature is revealed.

Recent studies on creativity have underscored these reflections. This creative person, the individual on whose vision progress has always depended, gives new life to the world. This seems, in part at least, to be so because he is open to all aspects of his personality. He balances masculinity and femininity, reason and passion, action and contemplation, and the other seemingly polarized aspects of the self. There is no way in which he *must be,* and so the richness of his inner possibilities is available to him. He is, as a result, more completely human and more flexible at the same time. He is not locked in the concrete of what is, and is therefore free to give his total energies to the achievement of his vision of what can be.

"You can observe a lot," Yogi Berra once said, "just by watching." The best evidence for the validity of these observations about the balance of feminine and masculine characteristics in mature persons rests in the genuine men and women all around us. An authentic man feels no urgency to apologize for his love of poetry, the opera, or the arts. He is not embarrassed at life's challenge to his tenderness and intuition. An authentic woman is able to compete and achieve without denying or betraying her femininity. She need not explain her strength or resiliency in the face of sorrow or disaster.

In some reflection of this we find Christ himself quite at

ease with the humanity he assumed so fully. He could spon-
taneously express the feminine component in his personality
by longing, like a mother hen, to protect his people. His full
manhood seems, in so many of his relationships, to bring out
the fullness of the women with whom he came in contact. St.
Paul mixes metaphors without apparent concern as he tries
to share all of himself with his converts. He is at one moment
a demanding father, but an instant later the mother who
gave them life in the Gospel.

Maturity of adjustment is not a matter of extremes. It is
rather a question of the mature balance of the inexhaustible
wealth of all that is human in every man and woman. This is
the creative font of mankind, the source of new life for the
world, and the model on which any deep understanding of
the People of God must be based.

4/ The Church as a Person

ANY analogy is as full of handicaps as it is of helps. The human person has, however, served long and well to give us some understanding of the Church. We have spoken of the Mystical Body and, in no less human terms, of the People of God. It seems clear that the use of these models invites us, first of all, to understand the human person and then to apply, as best we can, these insights in our appreciation of the Church itself.

If the Church can be thought of as a person, then we should expect it to exhibit the same signs of psychological maturity that we would look for in any individual. Indeed, the Church has recently manifested many of the behaviors of a person struggling for greater growth. As Charles Curran has pointed out, Vatican Council II had many of the features of the self-search of the counseling process. The words *council* and *counsel* have, in fact, a relationship in the basic meaning of "to take counsel with oneself." An individual enters a counseling relationship to survey himself, to look deeply at the roots of his behavior, in the hope that he will emerge with a more valid view of himself.

The person begins to look within himself instead of railing at the world around him. Rather than insisting that everyone else change, he senses that it is possible and also right to change himself. He must surrender any distorted view of himself that has hardened into a defense and become resistant to change. The individual must see himself as he is. He must open himself to the painful truth which will make him free. Redefining himself, he redefines his relationships to others; encrusted defenses fall, and he becomes more open in the whole range of his relationships. As he matures, he no longer needs to demand that reality should change to accommodate him.

This roughly describes the process begun by the Church in the momentous conciliar self-examination. Even now the effort for renewal is the extension of the Church's struggle for a more accurate self-concept, the painful journey to a truer self. The process of growth in a person requires that he be strong enough to endure self-disorganization in view of a healthier self-reorganization built on the truth. He has moments of doubt and confusion; even his friends wonder at what is occurring. Despite the suffering, however, there is the pervading sense that something healthy is going on.

Although this describes in some fashion the present struggle toward greater wholeness in the Church, it does not say that it is already accomplished. It suggests, rather, that following our analogy, growth will be a continuing process, built on sustained and deepening openness to the self. This openness, acquired as defenses diminish, is the absolute requirement for the action of the Holy Spirit. This openness to life as a process of growth in relationship to others is a major sign of maturity for the individual and for the Church. However, it demands of the Church the hardiness to tolerate the trembling process of self-reorganization.

This vital exploration of one's own depths is the inevitable challenge to the open person. So now the Church, breathed on by the Spirit, is entering into and understanding itself more clearly. Slowly, but in the long run surely, the Church is forming a new self-concept, a sounder one rooted in more deeply perceived truth.

As the process goes on, the Church must face its elements of masculinity and femininity. A healthy self-understanding demands an acceptance and an integration of these aspects of its existence in time. It is not too much to say that these dimensions of masculinity and femininity have been seriously out of balance in the past. Because of this the Church even now is not, in what we might term its "personality," as healthy as it should be. It is striking that the Church, described in the New Testament as the *New Creation,* and commissioned to *re-create* the face of the earth, has yet to achieve complete creative maturity.

Were we to offer a diagnosis we might suggest that the Church has been overmasculinized in its relationship to itself and to the world. It is badly in need of a redress of its male-female balance. We have within the Church a situation that could be described with the words of J. B. Priestley:

Where is the feminine principle, where is Woman in this madness? Where is the feminine emphasis here upon love, on the happiness of persons? . . . If I say, as I do, that a swing from the masculine to the feminine principle is now urgently necessary . . . I mean . . . that society itself must be as thoroughly permeated by womanliness as it is by masculinity, that *as a community,* not simply as separate persons, we must accept feminine values.

The People of God, the Christian Community celebrated by the liturgy: these are caricatures of what they could be if the elements of God's creation—male and female he made them—are not in a balanced and healthy relationship. The

Church does not find the truth of its being unless it faces the totality of its inner composition. It is thoroughly masculine and feminine. The balanced interplay of these elements is the source of its vitality and the guarantee of its continued growth. However, even as the patient in therapy, it must first sense and acknowledge the reality of its own selfhood. Otherwise, it will be stalled at an incomplete or distorted state of growth. The only mode of adjustment to itself or the world it is meant to serve will be defensive maneuvers. These protect a faulted view of the self through dynamics of denial or disguise. So, for example, an individual who will not look at his full self rationalizes his behavior. He gives a good reason for what he does. The only difficulty is that it is not the real reason. "I would have refused the bishopric anyway," the disappointed ecclesiastic says to cover his hurt. In the long run the person who employs these defenses as a major mode of adjustment fools only himself. He has built fatal flaws into his relationship to himself, and these carry over into his relationships with others.

The Church, through its human thinkers and administrators, has not as yet let itself look fully at its complete inner experience. Libraries have been filled with the manuscripts that have served to make its masculine self-image seem both reasonable and justified. If it has supposedly been a man's world, it has certainly been a man's Church as well. It has abounded in the attitudes and approaches of men who see only one side of themselves. Its defensiveness has been highlighted by the utter and complete canonical domination of the Church's women by its men. A woman, as one Church official once said to me, "is not capable of ecclesiastical jurisdiction, so the question of their place in the Church is settled." The more profound question as to why this has been so was left unattended. It was, I thought in that very minor moment of confrontation, as though this Church dignitary had not heard me. So, I believe, it has been for many centuries. The questions of feminine qualifications have not just been unanswered. They have received, to use Harry Stack Sullivan's splendid phrase, "selective inattention." This represents a classic defense that closes off reality to the individual who is not ready to face what a full view of reality would demand of him.

Endless examples of seeming prejudice against women by the male-oriented Church could be presented. Perhaps it is sufficient, to underscore the emotional component of the situation, to reflect on the frenzied rejoinders of some churchmen to the possibility of women priests. Any reason seems good enough to men anxious to close off the possibility of even thinking about this development. It is worth noting here that these overmasculine attitudes reflect something other than genuine manhood. They constitute a defensive distortion that has often been more neuter than manly. It is the kind of behavior one might expect of men who have never shaken off the skirtlike vesture of robes, frills, and flowing trains. Most priests and Church officials do not find these costumes very appealing. Unfortunately, a certain type of churchman not only likes but needs these outfits to blur his own uncertain self-identification.

In the same way, many examples of overmasculine approaches to the world of men could be also presented. Psychologically, these were inevitable, given the distorted or undeveloped picture the Church maintained of itself in the past. Nothing ever failed for Christendom like the crusades, the armored advances in the name of the Gospel. Nothing has failed more, in the long run, than the power-oriented manipulations of peoples in the name of truth. Nothing has failed more than the coercion and censorship that has all too often been substituted for trust and respect for the human race. The point of these reflections, however, is not to bewail the past but rather to emphasize the promise of this moment of potential openness by the Church to its feminine side. This is a hopeful time of growth for the Church as it lowers its defenses to face the fullness of its human membership.

The Church's inability to experience the fullness of its true self has had many consequences. Among them, for example, is the curious fact that overmasculinity has led to religious practice being considered a somewhat feminine thing. Churchgoing and the preservation of faith in families have in many places been disdained by men. They have preferred power and enterprise as their only respectable domain. This has been the fate of the Church in many lands, such as South America, where it came with cross and sword for conquest and conversion. Just as man cannot give life to himself, so overaggressive ecclesiastical enterprises, for all their muscularity, have also proved sterile.

It is also true that women, in reaction, have had to fight for rights that are really theirs in virtue of their own humanity. The struggle has been long and difficult because women have not been fully or freely accepted as human persons with a proper claim on all that this implies. Necessarily, women have been forced to use masculine means to make their way into the world of men. This has made many men even more anxious and defensive. It has contributed to the dynamics of uncertainty in men who have felt it necessary to shore up their challenged masculinity with subtler defenses. The developing sense of mutuality in male-female relationships has had many undertones of uneasiness. Only slowly have men and women been arriving at a more complete sense of openness and acceptance of one another. The perpetuation of the double standard, the theme that rights were being "granted" to women, the tension of conflict over the varying roles of men and women in society—these suggest that the overall question of their relationship in the common bond of humanity has at best been painfully and incompletely resolved.

The unfortunate result of the military atmosphere of the battle of the sexes has reinforced the mentality that women's rights are not theirs by birth but by masculine concession. This smacks of peace terms from generals embarrassed by defeat. Echoes of this are found in articles and symposia on the "place" or "role" of women in the Church. With what some churchmen feel as pardonable pride in their own willingness to yield up a portion of their patrimony, various niches and tasks are presented as appropriate for women. This goes counter to psychological and theological realities. Women are not to be granted rights; they possess them. Women are not to be given roles or tasks within the Church. They, as much as men, *are* the Church. If the concept of the People of God means what it must, then it is senseless to pursue the place of women in the Church along territorial dimensions. The sexes do not relate or blend within the Church as the result of truce talks.

The uncomfortable efforts to discover or create a role for the layman are another reflection of the highly restricted perception the Church has had of itself. It is not a problem of the Church's understanding the layman. The task is to understand man himself. The qualities of masculinity and femininity are not those of the hierarchy and religious but of the whole People of God. The time has come for the Church to broaden its view of what it really is. One concept that must be dropped is the incredible identification of its core with the relatively small cluster of clergy and religious who are only a part of the Church. The tasks and functions of laymen will only become clear after a basic realization that they are the Church as integrally as any other element.

This recognition and full growth of all that constitutes the People of God can only arise from within the organism. It must be ready to put aside the defenses which allow it to function without really examining itself.

The most heartening signs of the times are found in the fact that the Church is lowering its defenses and taking a long, hard look at itself. For centuries the basic posture toward itself and the world was defensive. For Catholic observers, Martin Luther had to be a lusty boor. All dissenters deserved the flames that often became their fate. Catholic doctrine, that last lucid light in a darkened world, had to be defended more than developed. But now, in the middle of the twentieth century, the Church has turned inward to begin to take counsel painfully with itself. The process is still underway but already the sloughed-off defenses are knee-deep in St. Peter's Square.

The remarkable thing that occurs when an individual discards his defenses is also occurring for the Church. The initial state of painful disorganization is not an easy burden. The person, however, in being able to approach himself, suddenly achieves something that no previous effort ever brought to him. He is more approachable by others. The ecumenical successes of this age have a partial psychological explanation in the reality of the Church's openness. With defenses put aside it achieves what it could never win by force. It is more easily approached by others. So too, it is more understanding of others. The ecumenical dialogue springs not so much from what the Church has done to or for other religions. It arises from what it has done to itself. The Spirit cannot fail to operate in the individual or the institution which gives up defenses.

The really hard look the Church must take is at the truth of its own composition. It is a people, men and women. It must be so revealed both to itself and to the whole world. There is no secure base for its redemptive mission aside from the complete truth about its own nature. If it is ever successfully to establish itself in a loving relationship with mankind, the Church must indeed commit itself to its inner human reality.

Such self-confrontation and commitment will require as much courage from the Church as it does from the individual person. "Human kind," according to T. S. Eliot, "cannot bear very much reality." The great expatriate poet catches some of the frailty of people who are caught in the coils of the human condition. It is easier to live in the shadow than grapple with the substance of life. It is no new temptation for men to look away from the strenuous tests of existence toward the sunlit fields of their dreams. When life and the burdens of continued growth seem excessive, the immature generally move sideways or backwards in their adjustment to reality. Drugs and alcohol offer long known escape routes. There are also less dramatic, if not less destructive, retreats into reverie or regressive behavior.

These responses that soften the impact of reality also diminish the personhood of those who choose them. Freud's illustration of regression is illuminating. The man who cannot face a new stage of life tries to go back, like a bedouin in the desert, to a former, comfortable encampment. The journey to full personal development, however, demands continuous forward movement. Fulfillment comes precisely from realizing more of our personal possibilities. The achievement of one stage of growth reveals itself as an invitation to move on to the next. The wise man knows that "you can't go home again" to the days that seem, in retrospect, appealingly innocent.

The People of God cannot go home again either, despite the widespread nostalgia for times of simpler faith and easier belief. Just as each man passes a line that removes him forever from childhood and adolescence, so the Church has passed into the times that test its maturity. The reassuring era of faith supported by supposedly solid and all-knowing structures has ended. The Church is suddenly left without the supports that allowed it to live for so long in its own world. The People of God are developing a firmer faith that flows from within themselves. This is, however, a difficult process of growth because the way is not clear ahead and the comfortable encampments of the past cannot be reentered.

This challenge to a truer and fuller development is furthered by the growth of the Church's men and women. It is their constant movement toward complete manhood and womanhood on which the continuing maturity of the Church depends.

If the day when Christ will be "all in all" is to dawn, it will be the result of the fidelity of each member of the People of God to attaining the perfection of his own personality. The issue of authentic manhood and womanhood is central to the unfolding of the mystery of the Church in this world. Nothing less than the achievement of all the growth possible is demanded from each person in the Church. The Church has no other source of growth and energy aside from its members. Although this growth is effected only by the action of the Spirit within them, it can be frustrated by their timidity or reluctance to acknowledge the realistic demands of their lives. The whole Church shrivels when its members turn their backs on the abundant challenges of life. The Mystical Body seems a shrunken and crippled wayfarer when its members reject the possibilities of what they could be in favor of the security of what they are. The principal occasion of this sees individual men and women failing to give themselves fully to their manhood or womanhood. The whole process of the Church's mission is inhibited, not so much by persecutors from without, as by the pusillanimous from within. The Church presents an incarnate community of love only when its members are grown fully enough to give themselves totally, trustingly, and together to the service of mankind. Adolescent men and women cannot give love enough by half to establish the Kingdom that is really a community.

Examples of undeveloped personalities are not difficult to observe. Neither are they difficult to accept and understand as long as they are not permanently shielding themselves from their fullest growth possibilities. When they have settled for intermediate stages of development, however, they have closed themselves to the action of the Spirit. They have, in effect, invalidated their instrumentality as sources of growth for the whole Church. Such are the selfish whose prize is power and the manipulation of others. Such are the childish who want liberal and frequent feeding and who are capable of distressful scenes when their needs are not immediately satisfied. Others who lack the energies of real love are the frightened ones who want the Church to be a protective enclosure in a wild and wicked world. The effete and the effeminate flourish in a tragic travesty of worship that is built on narcissistic ceremonial.

Still others are the men and women who blanch at the first discomforting reality in their lives. Rather than confront themselves in the face of contradiction or disappointment, they withdraw and walk away. The dynamism of their lives is their own need, whether that need is to be liked or just to be left alone. Unfortunately, they have never come to face and forego their own needs, to empty themselves of self-concern in order to serve the needs of others. Half the time they are unaware that they are in the grip of their own self-centeredness. Their knowledge of themselves is incomplete and, consequently, so too is a proper love of themselves. They have no gift of themselves to offer to their fellowmen. In the end, like the Gospel hirelings who take flight in times of danger, they spend their powers in trying to save themselves.

I once witnessed a clear example of this in the response of a young clergyman to a widow who was standing by her dead husband's coffin. She was weeping. Why shouldn't she weep, their forty-five years together now ended? The cleric was reaching out a hand and whispering, "Now don't cry, don't cry." What he was really saying, although he did not fully understand it himself, was, "If you don't cry, I won't feel so bad. If you don't cry, I won't feel so self-conscious and uneasy. If you don't cry, I won't feel so helpless in the face of your grief." She had a right to something better from her clergyman than the reassurances that were aimed at himself and his own needs. Granting the imperfections of human nature, it is evident that he badly needed more of his manhood to face and share the reality of her sorrow. The world of men, full of fears and pain, has a right to the human response of men and women adult enough to understand and enter into its grief. It has a right to the kind of redemptive relationship that can only come from the fully grown.

Any failure of manhood or womanhood on the part of priests or religious deeply affects the quality of saving relationships they are capable of making with those who are in their care. The Spirit cannot fully inform relationships that have fundamental distortions or obstacles built into them. That is why the image of the priesthood, religious life, and apostolic works of any kind are at the mercy of the immature. It is worthwhile, in the light of current theological emphasis, to speculate on whether the effects of the sacraments themselves are linked to the degree of maturity of those who administer and receive them. The sacramental ministry of holy orders and the sacramental sharing of matrimony provide clear examples for our consideration. The great channels of grace for the human family remain the human mediators of the gospel truths. If they have not freed themselves from the obstacles to growth within themselves, they cannot effectively bring life and truth to others.

The process of an individual's growth is deeply involved with the persons with whom he lives or interacts. Parents must provide a model of sure personal identification or the developing pattern of manhood or womanhood is vague and uncertain. The conflicts and crises of growth are resolved through appropriate relationships with the parents. The relationship between the husband and wife is of great significance in the healthy raising of their offspring. Their love for each other, which acquires new dimensions through the years, enables them to free their children for lives of their own. The whole complex of extra-familial relationships with friends, teachers, and religious figures provides the enriched environment of healthy personal identification for the young man or woman. Beyond this, men and women must meet anew and discover the true depths of their masculinity and femininity in mature and realistic relationships.

These are the inescapable interpersonal elements of successful self-identity for every human being. The full measure of growth in Christ Jesus is attained in no other context. This is the kind of growth demanded of all the men and women in the Church. Great openness and a commensurate willingness to yield up all personal obstacles to growth make this possible. It is with this realization of the Church's need for fully developed men and women that the reflections of the following chapters are presented.

II/GROWTH IN THE SPIRIT

5 / The Male Mystique

THERE was a sadness beyond singing of it in Ernest Hemingway's suicide. This great grizzly man had thumped his chest at life, struggled with the beasts in the sea and on safari; he had celebrated the matador's moment of truth but met his own with the sure proof of his manhood still eluding him. You can hardly think of him except in the rough clothes of the adventurer, squinting under some far distant sun, seeking the experience that would confirm for him what nobody else questioned. The elaborate armor of the outdoor man never quieted the fears of the inner man. If, however, he is the most famous of men who needed constant proof of their virility, he is by no means the only one.

A fully blown mystique of masculinity has developed in our culture where "the symbols of maleness", as Alan Watts has observed, "are confused with genuine maleness." The phenomenon has many faces in this land where the trappings of manhood are mass-produced and marketed for any man who is even slightly anxious about his sexual identity.

Marriage manuals seem to have a fecundity of their own as they spread their clinically enticing tables of contents across the pages of the family sections of the Sunday papers.

To the fascinated and uneasy male, they promise prowess unto a biblically fruitful old age. That so many books offer so much to so many people suggests that their publishers have tapped a genuine vein of uncertainty and have found it to be made of gold. The motivational analysts long ago discovered that the least likely products can be sold with similar appeals. A red convertible can be endowed with the appeal of a red-gowned seductress for the longing adolescent man. Let the same diminished male ego identify with the archetypical impersonality of John Wayne's cowboy hero or the vindictive Marshal of Dodge City and he will be further reassured about his own unforgiving masculine fibre.

Professional football provides bone-crunching and bloody violence and, while this may drain off aggressive impulses for the many, it also provides vicarious manliness for those who need it. After all, real men do like and understand this sport, but their ranks have recently been swelled by those who value chiefly the symbol of attending the game. They may not be able to tell a fullback from a forward pass, but their blood seems to them to run a little redder when they find themselves in the fine male environment of the stadium on Sunday afternoon.

A staggering hard sell is currently underway to market traditionally feminine products and services, such as cosmetics and hair styling, on the premise that they enhance the purchaser with a maddening masculinity. Stamp *007* on them, and everything from trenchcoats to toilet water will work the same wonders for the uneasy male who is standing at the counter, his money growing hot in his hand, ready to buy ready-made manhood. A grotesque zenith has been reached in the idealization of the manhood of James Bond, cool, uncaring, and incapable of any deep human relationship; here is the real man, "fighting, fornicating, and fugitive," the hollow and desperate hero who is no man at all.

Perhaps there is nothing really new in this traffic in mail order masculinity; perhaps our culture has just become more sophisticated in catering to the needs of men who are not fully grown. After all, sex has always sold well, and throughout history fearful males have purchased an unconscionable variety of elixirs and advice. Hugh Hefner is not the newest but, because he styles himself a savant, only the saddest entrepreneur of the symbols of virility. If we must accept the reality of generations of men as desperate as Don Juan himself to prove their manliness, we must not let the issue of the roots of real manhood remain at this superficial level. Above all, we must not allow the discussion of important issues within the Church to be obscured by the miasma of this far reaching mystique. Curiously enough, the seeds of this same difficulty have been sown into recent discussions of celibacy and seminary training.

A source of much wonderment are the advertisements for religious orders, laced with the theme "If you want to be a real man, join us. . . ." This is the psychological packaging that sells the symbols of manhood and, unfortunately for the religious groups that use it, it can appeal only to the needy.

Far more disturbing, however, is the tenor of much that has been written on the subject of celibacy in Catholic periodicals during the last year. Serious questions must be raised in the light of the sense of values that is apparently involved in much of the discussion. It is high time for the Church to confront the questions of chastity and celibacy, but shallowness of understanding has characterized too much of the public discussion thus far. The male mystique, the symptom of uncertain manhood, is surely present on the one hand, just as an equally superficial juridical approach is present on the other. But the real values involved center on the deepest aspects of interpersonal relationships, on the well-springs of human growth and maturity, on the root meaning of love among men, on the existential possibilities of all that life can and should mean.

The male mystique is clearly revealed in the letters and articles, many written by priests, which have called for a change in celibacy so that priests can experience the love of a woman that will make them whole. Repeatedly the theme is raised; I am a man and I need a woman to fulfill me as a man and, therefore, I should be free to have a woman who can do this for me. The anguish of these writers is as real as their intensely personal words, but many are dangerously close to prizing woman, not for herself, but for what she can symbolize in masculine fulfillment. What they confine themselves to voicing, whether they intend it that way or not, is the incredibly typical male position of thinking only of what women can do for them. What view of woman, one might ask, is inherent in arguments that center principally on their usefulness in answering men's needs for fuller manhood? What attenuated personalistic philosophy is betrayed by a viewpoint that regards so little the needs and rights and role of women themselves?

Perhaps this is the "in" thing to make one feel like a man in the age of aggiornamento: woman completes man, so give us what completes us. Surely these discussants do not deliberately cast woman in a utilitarian role. Rather, they seem naive about the meaning of persons, as if they were not at all conscious of marriage as a sharing of life, in considerable pain, by a man and woman who reach into the depths of each other's being, complementing but costing each other constantly, fulfilling but draining each other as well. It is this apparent lack of appreciation of the true meaning of mature love between the sexes that invalidates much of the recent discussion.

Many of those who have been vocal about celibacy view marriage as a solution for what they may be accurately describing as the unfulfilled manhood of the priest. This attitude of a taker of what a woman can give to make him a man can only belong to someone who is not yet ready for marriage, much less any other kind of grown-up relationship with other persons. The safe half-formed philosophy lies beneath the current enthusiasm of some educators for "dating" among seminarians. The idea seems to be, and what an agony of emptiness it reveals, that the proponents have missed something somewhere along the line and that they feel this loss intensely. It is probably true that semi-cloistered seminarians, if there are such still, miss something when they cut themselves off from healthy contacts with their own world. It is appalling, however, to advocate that girls should be dated, should be "used"—if you can stand the truth of the matter, on a temporary basis to satisfy personal experiential lacunae in the lives of future priests.

Simply stated, women are not present in the world for heterosexual experimentation or self-justification at any level in life; they are not around just to insure that we will feel more like men. "Well, we don't mean that," the advocates of dating will say, but they have already missed the point. To relate to women solely for what they can do for us is not really much more profound than the philosophy of Hugh Hefner. It is relationship without commitment to another person, it is symbiotic and selfish, and it is unworthy of Christian consideration. The scandal is the insensitivity to the real value of persons that these self-styled "personalists" betray. The process of healthy growth in humans is not mechanical, and persons are not disposable parts. The discovery of the meaning of love, the love that gives life and growth, the kind of love strong enough to answer the needs of anguished men, will never be understood by men who seem to have no realization of its complex and crushing demands. Real love is seeded with pain; its counterpoint is found in the epic rhythms of death and resurrection, of gaining only by giving all; and while it inspirits man, it takes the breath out of him as well.

There is, of course, another side to this coin, of more ancient and more rigid imprint. It is a sad truth that the conditions of priestly and religious life almost make it impossible for people to experience the meaning of real love. If the solution does not lie in some kind of mutual exploitation to provide preprofession sex, it is easy to see that excesses in this direction have been largely a reaction to the unconvincing accumulation of arguments adduced by a squeaky clean generation of writers to glorify virginity. Many articles are written by commentators who obviously have never really understood human beings; it is equally difficult to believe that they understand much about God.

To preserve virginity like a shrunken and fragile treasure under shatterproof glass, with the other virtues clustered about it like well-armed but apprehensive museum guards, is to store a relic that no longer moves the world. It is to distort its meaning, to make an end in itself of antiseptic removal from human relationships; this devotion to the desiccation of the human spirit becomes blasphemous when it is alleged that this kind of virtue is eminently pleasing to God. Neither is it a good time to justify virginity on the grounds that it frees us to devote ourselves more fully to our work. Even the most casual and unbiased observer of our apostolic efforts is not willing to buy that any more. Being a virgin does not,

of itself, make you work harder; there is no sudden sublimation of energies on a grand scale into the good works of God.
Were this true, the world would be a smouldering ruin
from the unleashed action of the Spirit. As it is, our work
progresses pretty much apace, and wherever the real action
is in the world, in General Motors or the General Assembly,
married people are managing things. The illusion that marriage interferes with dedication, productivity, and/or true
greatness in loving our fellowmen should be dispelled forever.

Nor can anyone be deeply impressed by the claim that,
when we are virginal, we are automatically freed to love
more people more fully. The theory is fine; it is only the
reality of our practice that gives the lie to it. In fact, we do
not immediately love others more, and half the time we do
not love each other at all. Well, then, they say, celibacy is an
"eschatological sign" because it demonstrates the kind of
life, without marriage, that will be ours in Heaven. Nothing
more perfectly illustrates the point I am making than this
blandly offered argument. The authentic eschatological sign
is not the celibate but the person, whoever he or she is, who
loves other people truly. A genuine and deep celibate love,
one that reaches out to accept and understand and to give
the gift of self to another, the root phenomenon of loving
someone else as a human person—this is the sign, just as it
is also the sign by which all men will know that we are
Christ's disciples.

The basic problem is the existential one of learning to
love other human beings humanly, fully, and unselfishly.
This only occurs when we truly entrust ourselves to others,
when we care for them, when we experience the sacredness
of some other who deeply trusts and believes in us. You do
not have to be married to experience this, but you will not
be married long if you do not experience it. This is the

solemn and vital dimension of interpersonal values which is paid equal disservice by uncertain men who want women's gifts without giving themselves and by the sterile inhumanists whose ideal for religious life is one gigantic chess match in which the pieces are preserved inviolate by a complicated set of rules, the first of which says that the game is never to be played in the first place.

Priests and religious, like all normal persons, can grow only in the context of rich and real personal relationships. Fundamentally, the task for them is no different than it is for any other human being; they must learn to love others as persons, for their sake, and this love fails if it is exploitative and self-aggrandizing quite as much as when it is vacuum-packed and self-protective. It has often been noted that the priesthood and religious life can offer ideal conditions for relationships that are, in the phrase of Harry Stack Sullivan, "fleeting and fugitive". Legalisms, all too often proclaimed under the legend "the will of God" inscribed on a banner so stiffly starched that it yields to no listing of the Spirit, tend to canonize superficial, but oh, so safe, personal relationships. It is difficult for healthy lay people to believe that anybody could seriously debate the place of real friends in life, but over and over again this question is raised in journals directed toward members of religious groups. It is hardly any wonder that some priests and religious feel that they have missed something and invoke the male mystique or the excesses of exaggerated personalism in their human relationships.

For example, as a supervisor of priest-counselors over a number of years, I have noticed that priests who study counseling respond warmly to its insights and generously try to implement them in their pastoral work. They get to be good "beginning counselors," that is, they can start therapeutic relationships in a genuinely helpful way. They have learned to withhold blithe advice and they open themselves to listen to what the troubled person has to say. In the cathartic initial sessions of counseling they can stay out of the way and the other person, anxious to express his or her emotional problems, shoulders the responsibility for what is said in the interview. It is after three or four meetings that difficulties begin for the counselor because now the burden of the burgeoning relationship must be shared by both parties. Now the counselor must be a full person, open to himself and to the other person; here is the territory of which he is unsure and here it is that he can falter.

The priest-counselor is not accustomed to relationships that make such existential demands on him, he is unused to working through a human relationship where his only equipment is his own personality. This is the very point, then, when he senses that this other person is willing to believe in and trust him, that causes him uneasiness. He is far more comfortable doing things for others than in being someone for them; he is far more at ease in brief relationships which cost only time and energy than in those which cost him something of his real self. His life as a priest can, in fact, be filled with brief encounters, and this is not to deny that he does good in these. It is to observe rather that his attitude toward human relationships can be like one of the Rothschilds toward the stock market—"like a cold shower: quick in and quick out."

The priest tends to withdraw from relationships that demand more of him than his training and conditions of life have prepared him to give. Human relationships for priests like this are necessarily short-term investments from which he would like a quick profit with little risk-taking involved. At this critical point in the counseling relationship, when he must let himself out to the other person, the priest may find the challenge one for which his resources have run out. This is the time when, if the relationship is to be health-giving, the therapist must respond by growing himself. Now, trust of and commitment to this other concrete individual must be more than bywords; now is the bone and marrow of the priest's own person involved, and he might get hurt. This is what a genuine human relationship demands—the presence of our person, exposed and vulnerable, the loving gift of self to another human person.

Too many priests and religious get defensive at this point and they can find the best reasons in the world to be cautious. "After all, this person should see a professional." "I should refer this case to a psychiatrist." Any reason is a good reason when we are incapable of continuing in a relationship in which someone trusts and believes in us and we must respond in kind. The priest who cannot give at this level, who cannot sense in his innards the challenge to his own development that is involved, is not yet mature enough to understand either marriage or celibacy. Only the priest who has plumbed the depths of relating to a flesh-and-blood kinsman in the human condition and learned to give without possessing and to enter the world of the other, willing to pay the personal cost of reverencing this other's personality; only he has learned that real love is full of pain, that genuine maturity is hard-bought, and that this is at the core of understanding life itself. Only the man who has not experienced this could look on marriage as a solution for his problems, at dating as a forward step in seminary training, or at women as feminine conveniences for our fulfillment.

For too long celibacy and chastity have been presented in terms of the tension between the spirit and the flesh, as though this struggle for self-control summed up the meaning of the virtue. For an equally long time marriage has been viewed as a relaxation of that tension, a near nirvana of conjugal bliss. Neither celibacy nor marriage is done justice by this all too prevalent caricature; the issues involved are the same for both of these conditions of life because they turn on an appreciation of the deep personal demands that loving another makes on us. Real love is full of living and dying; it is a long-term investment that takes the best that a person is because it takes all that a person is.

The understanding of marriage or religious vows is not possible for people who are insensitive to the deep demands of sharing themselves with others. Marriage is an invitation to give to another person, for better, for worse, for richer, for poorer, yes, in sickness and in health. Togetherness is not deep enough a sentiment to sustain two people through their years with each other. Celibacy and the vow of chastity are invitations to the same kind of giving, to the same kind of gift of self to others, an invitation to pain and growth, to death and resurrection, in loving concrete persons, undefensively and nonpossessively. The Spirit is the source for all lovers, and his flames gutter out in personalities that are too shallow or too closed off out of fear.

If the Church and its teachers have had one truth to preserve through the ages, it is a realistic vision of the human family, an understanding of the person as the center of life and its meaning. If the law and the prophets are summed up in love, and if loving our neighbor is the only command Christ left us, then the Church is the guardian of the only truths that can make us free. God is indeed dead when men have forgotten the meaning of each other, when they have died themselves because the Spirit has been supplanted by the supposed symbols of his presence. But empty symbols will never do in a world that is weary and hungry and yearning in a thousand disfigured and disguised ways for real love.

If, as Wordsworth says, some thoughts are too deep for tears, then this whole issue of maturely entering into the meaning of love within the Church is too deep for the mindless discussions reflected in the ecclesiastical brand of the male mystique. Neither will the Church understand its own vocation of preserving and teaching the real meaning of love from the pronouncements of stiff-stocked puritans who live at a remove from mankind. The real questions are still largely unsuspected by these two latter groups. Let them look at life and hopefully learn what it is all about.

The Church cannot afford to fail in confronting the many internal confusions that have obscured its understanding of the most profound sign of its quickening by the Spirit. This can only be done by grown-up men with real senses of values, men scarred by living, men seared and matured by the flames of the Spirit. These are the men who understand other men and something of the God who is Love, and they will be the agents of the world's redemption.

The world, to which we promise life, and that to the full, deserves something better from us than the superficialities and platitudes so easily mouthed by the loveless and the unloving. We have to face the problem of human love, in marriage and religious life, as the action of the Spirit in uniting men and we have to take a close and unblinking look at the institutional obstructions that have hobbled the Spirit and impoverished us at the same time. This is a difficult task, perhaps the most basic of all tasks, because if its implications for all the world's present wounds of war, race relations, and population problems. It is a staggering task but it is *the* task and, despite the immense difficulties and defenses involved, "the time has come to begin."

6/The Women
Who Are More Than Poor

ANYBODY'S lexicon of Catholic clichés has had to make room recently for a bright newcomer: the fondness we have exhibited for discussing everything "in the light of Vatican II." But many earnest and unprejudiced observers find themselves in a postconciliar penumbra, if not total darkness. Peter's ship has set sail, not with a carefully charted map at sunlit high noon, but with the most general of directions into the fast-falling night. The crew members are not cursing the darkness or just failing to comprehend the light. They realize that the anxious voyage is bringing them into the real world, toward the ports of call where mankind truly dwells.

Healthy Christians, living in the darkness of Vatican II, realize that wholeness involves struggle just as surely as growth involves pain. So, too, they understand that love unfeigned encompasses suffering, and maturity invites into their lives the uncertainty of obscured horizons as a constant condition. It is because the Church, together with everyone in it, is growing up, that we find pain in our lives today. This is the great sign of life, not of imminent death—and we can be grateful for it.

Christians sense that they are involved in salvation history, and that risks run high in the story of the redemption of the world. They realize that whatever can be a step forward can also be a step backward. Are there, they ask, words more haunting than these said by the Jesuit Superior General, Father Arrupe: "I am afraid that we may repeat yesterday's answers to tomorrow's problems, talk in a way men no longer understand. . . . If we do this, we shall more and more be talking to ourselves; no one will listen, because no one understands what we are trying to say."

Although the Church is front-page news, the reality of religion's message to man seems to be becoming remote. Stanley Frost, for example, has noted that for modern Western man, ". . . churchgoing is a leisure time activity, and thus a 'play' phenomenon." Wise men and guiding stars can only be credited in a make believe world, and he concludes, ". . . as the wise men . . . are not 'real,' so, too, the Incarnation is not 'real' either. Both can have their place only in that other world, the world of the illogical, the irrational, the unreal."

The healthiest effect of this tumultuous age is the invitation it has given to priests and religious to break the barriers which keep them in the realm of the unreal. This challenges their institutions and their hearts but it is a good thing because the future of the good news to which they have given their lives depends on their response. Everywhere priests and religious are being forced to enter into the experience of their brothers and sisters in the Mystical Body, to shoulder the same burdens that are their daily lot in the struggle to lead good lives.

If religion is going to be real to a people that is ravening for it, it will be because we priests and religious are real, because we have been able to put away our playthings, let our dreams die, and enter fully into the human condition. Never have we been so challenged to embrace humanity, to become fully incarnate in relationship to mankind. This is what renewal of the religious life is all about. We have been urged, by the times themselves, to take our place in the grown-up world and to live by its substantial values. A good deal of our present-day pain flows from the fact that we have no choice but to taste the common experience of most persons. Religious profession is made to persons, not to practices; our lives are given over to caring about, not just being wary of, the fundamental values of life itself. A life of faith is meant to be a mystery but not so mysterious that it is lived in any other world but the anxious and pain-filled one into which God sent his only Son.

We are facing the kinds of problems the people of God have to face every day, the kinds of problems that can be understood and solved only by those who are ready and able to grow in real love. The great compelling Christian sign ought to be love, and this incredibly scarce commodity is full of ups and downs and ins and outs. That is how we find it in the world of struggling Christians around us, in that world where people must love in order to give life. It is chiefly a world of husbands and wives, with all the hazards humanity is heir to: disappointments and sudden deaths; giving of the self in order to feed, clothe, and educate children; sons and husbands dying half a world away in the clouded struggle of Vietnam; sick children, sleepless nights, and seemingly endless sacrifice. It is not a wicked world of pleasure. It is the world of countless millions struggling to raise their families and lower their debts—the world we are called to redeem.

The crystalline walls of the sanctuary known as religious life have been splintered into shards, and religious find themselves exposed to the terrible responsibility of truly adult Christian living. The choice is clear: either they live more fully than ever or they will die more surely and quickly than can be imagined. We are forced, thank God, to lead grown-up lives, with a grown-up sense of values; and, if this has been a long time coming, our acceptance of it cannot be a long time delayed.

This is the kind of experience that many seminary professors have recently traumatically undergone. They have discovered that the process of helping seminarians can no longer be carried out from afar. They have had to relinquish their Victorian book-lined studies. They have sensed that nothing grows unless you love it but, at the same time, they have found the demand love makes on them to be a harrowing experience. Rudely jolted into the real world of living and dying and caring, it is not strange that they have felt like the professors who went out in the cold; but it is strange, indeed, that men who knew the philosophy and theology of love did not know much about love itself.

Unfortunately, many religious groups have missed the meaning of the pain and anxiety that they have suddenly found filling their lives. They have failed to read the signs of the times and they remind one of the groups of zealots who, a century ago, moved out into the wilderness, proclaiming the imminent end of the world. But the world kept turning and prospering, and while these fanatics preserved their enclave, the sun rose on a new age. Busy still with their butter churns and spinning wheels, they are regarded as quaint curios of a bygone time. So it is with many religious groups who kept busy in the enclave of their worrisome little worlds while the sun rose on the secular city.

Many of the old models of the religious life are spent of their usefulness. The religious life, as it has been lived, is in many places in an advanced state of disintegration. Those groups bent on resurrecting it intact are like spiritualists trying to materialize a ghost. The greatest of present-day tragedies is not the agony of rebirth that we all share but the blindness of many who fail to see the position we are in. The greatest danger is not that the dust will never settle, but that it will—on our eyes, so that we will never achieve the vision that is necessary today. The task is not just to quiet our own anxiety or to come in out of the cold, but to strike out, under the guidance of the Spirit, in healthy new directions in the religious life. Religious life needs renewal and adaptation, and the Church has provided broad guidelines for these, but it more urgently needs rethinking and reformulation. Religious life needs to evolve in a wholesome way, and the great challenge is to be a living part of this for the sake of the whole Church.

Religious women are faced with the very difficult challenge to grow up as women in the Church, to bring the fullness of their womanhood to the Church which is so in need of it. They are, it has been remarked, much in the position of the Negro, who has been told by a paternalistic and prospering society that if he remains a child, he will be cared for—but on the horrendous condition that he exist only to add a touch of minstrel charm to life and should not aspire to be a man. He can serve and he will even be regarded with affection but he cannot grow up. The white man does not like his claim on humanity. In great groaning pain, the Negro has rejected this proposition and he tells us why he "can't wait;" he flexes the muscle of "black power" and speaks of "the fire next time."

So the sister is prized by a paternalistic and prospering Catholic society as a little girl, innocent and virginal, smiling sweetly, sacrificing silently, just human enough for the mindless caricatures of a dozen motion pictures. But the subtle admonitions remain: be a child and do not aspire to be a fully grown woman; take care of our children and teach them their prayers; grow weary, grow old, but don't grow up. It takes great courage, the kind of patient strength women have, to face the challenge and not be frightened off by it. The Church's women must be fruitful virgins and faithful wives, not for the pleasant poetry of these phrases, but for the rock-bottom reality of their vocation in the Church. They must risk rejection and misunderstanding in bringing the adult feminine dimension into the personality of the Church. Their sense of values must be such that the world, even our Catholic world, will readjust to their relevance. They must shatter the image of religious who play a game of life that is isolated from the human condition. For they are isolated no longer, and this is why they "can't wait" either. There could be "the fire next time" for the Church too, and it could be the holocaust instead of the light of the world.

Christian womanhood is the life of the "new nun," and the full realization of this is vitally important for them and all the Mystical Body. I am convinced that the dedicated women of the Church can present, as few others could, the model of full-grown Christian femininity to all mankind, and in company with priests and brothers can strikingly contribute to the renewal of the face of the earth.

Theologians, striving to understand Christ's embrace of humanity, have emphasized recently just how fully and deeply he took on our flesh. He was not an automaton, somebody who just looked like a man but operated always from his divine knowledge, not just a figure of humanity knowledgeably going through preordained paces. He was so fully human that he allowed himself the full measure of the human condition. He did not just pretend to learn, or to be tired, or to suffer the agonies of gradually realizing his messianic role. A slowly developing awareness of his salvific mission burgeoned in him, a growth following the laws of humankind opened him, in his humanity, to the fullness of his Sonship. If he so thoroughly entered the human condition and let himself be subject to it, learning obedience through the things he suffered, then Mary's influence on him precisely as a man—the influence of a full woman—must be looked at anew. She gave her child life and love and prepared him as a flesh-and-blood, feeling human being for the immensity of his sacrificial vocation. Her influence was deeply and thoroughly human. Theologians are making clear the importance of Mary's human role as woman and mother to her child. Her titles are more than honorific, and her deep human interaction with her son flowed from the full realization of her fruitful virginity.

A recent interpretation of the exchange between mother and son at the wedding feast at Cana underscores this dimension of Mary's vocation. In as human a setting as can be thought of, Mary is seen, not as the woman who misunderstood her son, but as the mother who, open and sensitive to the needs of others, acted as the human agent in opening him as well. Perhaps this is the real miracle of Cana, a clear revelation of woman's vital importance in the Church.

Women who are fully grown bring themselves into relationship with men in the Church in a balanced and lifegiving way. It is the kind of relationship that is neither overly romantic nor sentimental, because it demands a mature response from both man and woman. If Mary's influence on the growth of her son cannot be ignored, neither can Joseph's. In truth, the loving relationship between Mary and Joseph must be perceived as the strongest factor in the development of the manhood of Jesus. Mary and Joseph, no less than any other parents, constituted the human formative setting in which Christ grew up. Nazareth was not just mother and son. This is an enormous distortion of the fact that the mystery of Christ's manhood can only be grasped if the picture is filled out realistically. Christ grew in relationship to both Mary and Joseph. Their relationship to each other, their bond of sacrificial celibate love, was the human source of his balanced manhood. The young maiden and the vigorous carpenter loved each other deeply, and the Spirit flowed fully in them through their relationship. They needed each other, and Christ the man needed them both. The Spirit comes to the Church when its men and women can relate to each other in the same mature way.

Recent articles have speculated on the real place of sisters in the Church. But their great role is to bring womanhood into the Church. All their other services will flow from this. This is a meaningless notion, however, unless real manhood is also present to complete the relationship. Man and woman in the Church cannot be thought of separately any more than Mary and Joseph can. It is their mature interaction that opens the People of God to the action of the Spirit. Sisters can be found anywhere, even at wedding feasts, but only in a meaningful way if there is the possibility that they can be equal sharers with men in the redemptive tasks of the Church.

Men and women in-Spirit each other. They breathe life into one another so that each can live a vocation of service to God's People with their complete manhood and womanhood. This is not accomplished by perpetuating the dominance of women by men. Neither is it furthered by re-creating the atmosphere of the battle of the sexes. This is a battle that cannot be won, although it can have tragic consequences for both sides. Woman's call is to completed personhood in the

Church. This demands a healthy relationship with the men who also serve the Church.

What are some of the implications of this for the problems of renewal?

Sisters cannot be women to the Church from afar. They must bring their womanhood into the human encampments of the pilgrim Church. The conditions of their lives must be the normal and healthy ones necessary for the growth of full women. They are not called to be deferential servants or little girls but grown-up women who are unafraid of their femininity. Any aspect of the religious life which diminishes or stunts the development of healthy women must be put aside. This is not an invitation to anarchy or a shapeless life. It is rather a call to a life whose discipline flows from its purpose, whose sacrifice comes, not from petty frustrations, but from bringing salvation in the human condition.

An end must be put to renewal discussions that center only on the horarium or an end will be put to these superficial discussants. Any practices that preserve childhood or childish attitudes in the lives of professed sisters must be abandoned or their religious houses will soon be abandoned too. The Church has dramatically underscored the freedom of the adult person and, in a sense, is challenging all of us to become Christians. Women need respect and privacy; they need the conditions that allow them to grow in a healthy way from within, and the freeing of this growth is the principal charge of those in authority. Authority, as has been noted, means "to make able to grow," and sister superiors are called to be "increasers" rather than "controllers." They must see that their sisters have life and have it to the full. Their own sense of values will be tested in this enterprise, and it cannot be less than adult at this time in history.

In this regard, no matter what the cost in public or private agonies, sisters will have to deal with the problem of mass institutionalization, the difficulties of which have been mentioned often enough. Women are simply not made to live together by the hundreds, and the human cost of preserving these conditions will eventually be so high that no religious group will be able to pay it. Practical economic necessity seems so often to demand it, but the model for the religious life is not the team or the Pentagon, but the family and the home. Artificially created communities are not communities at all and they will never become such merely by urging, wishing, or even praying. Mass institutions slowly put to death people who are meant for a full life.

The concept of the religious family, with its multiple relationships within and without, is dear to all religious and is currently the subject of much discussion and hopeful experimentation. There is concern, as well, especially regarding the personal aspect of the professional relationships of religious men and women in the Church. The Spirit was at work in the founding of religious communities, and it would be difficult to deny that many founders of men's groups were made the more sensitive to his promptings because of their healthy relationships with women.

In Church history we read constantly of women who stood always at the side of great men, helping them, reassuring them, opening them to the possibilities of their service of mankind. St. Francis de Sales and St. Ignatius head a list that is familiar to all. In the modern day I am personally aware of the profound relationship between Bishop James Anthony Walsh and Mother Mary Joseph in the growth of Maryknoll. But there is also Teilhard de Chardin who wrote throughout his adult life, from the shelter of the trenches to the final shelter of his grave, to his beloved cousin. Charles de Foucauld maintained, from his desert hut, a constant correspondence with a woman relative in Paris. Recently the translation of the letters written by Jordan of Saxony to Diana, the Dominican nun, in the 13th century have revealed how important she was in his growth and accomplishments.

All these truths, sensed keenly by young religious and priests throughout the world, have made thoughtful observers reflect on the deeper cooperation that is needed between men and women in the Church today. Alert to dangers, they are also more alert to the rich possibilities and importance of God's chosen men and women working more closely than has been fashionable or possible in recent years. They are called to help the Church have life, and this demands, in the unfolding dimensions of celibate consecration, that they give life to one another.

In a sense that is not sentimental, men and women in the Church stand in mature need of each other more than ever. Otherwise they will never reach the goals God has for them. Otherwise they will never reveal the full meaning of the Church even to themselves.

Vatican II's *Lumen Gentium*, which sees the Church as the mystery of the People of God, finds, as it should, a reflection of this truth in the families of religious communities: men and women working together for the sake of the Kingdom. In these families different gifts are needed and different roles have to be filled, and here again woman is indispensable. Priests and sisters share the prophetic and pastoral charge, but without the attitude of openness to the Spirit which their interrelationship brings, neither can live their vocation fully.

Something of this relationship is reflected in the relationship between Word and Spirit. The flavor of what I am trying to say is caught in the passage on the Spirit and the Word in *Vocabulaire de Théologie Biblique:*

Throughout the Old Testament, the Spirit and the Word of God continuously act together. If the Messiah is able to fulfill the Word of the Law . . . it is because he has the Spirit; if the prophet witnesses to the Word, it is because the Spirit has seized him; if the Servant is able to bring the Word of salvation to the nations, it is because the Spirit rests upon him; if Israel one day can adhere in its heart to this Word, it will only be in the Spirit. Though inseparable, the two powers do have distinct characteristics. The Word penetrates from the outside . . . ; the Spirit flows and infuses itself imperceptibly. The Word makes itself known and heard; the Spirit remains invisible. The Word is revelation; the Spirit interior transformation. The Word stands forth, erect and subsistent; the Spirit comes down, spreads about, sinks into. This apportioning of roles and yet their necessary association are found again in the New Testament: the Word of God made flesh by the activity of the Spirit does nothing without the Spirit, and the completion of his work is the gift of the Spirit.

The work of the Church cannot be accomplished without an ever-deepening sharing of the vocation of men and women within it. There is something men give, when they are real men, and also something women give, when they are real women, which makes for the fullness of the Church. Who will sensitize the People of God to where the Spirit hovers over the world; who will help them to sense depths within themselves still beyond their own understanding, if not the men and women who open themselves to the Spirit through the gift of themselves to the Church? Who will help women to grow fully, as Mary was helped by Joseph, if not men? This is the awesome aspect of this relationship in faith, but it will be realized only if men and women are able to deepen their relationship in person.

Now this is full of possible difficulties—and real ones as well—and they must be discussed together. This theme will be enlarged on in the next chapter but it is obvious that our students, servants of the Church but still in their years of formation, sense the climate of talk about masculine and feminine fulfillment that so fills the air today. And yet it is not always clear that their understanding of these concepts is as mature as we might desire. Of course, we cannot expect full growth from those who are still growing, but even those of us who most deeply cherish the ideal of the Church's family sometimes wonder what is going on.

What I am saying is that I do not believe that we further our cooperation best, as the men and women of the Church, through the agency of our students. Neither do I think we can turn our backs on the present age, withdraw behind our respective walls, and feel that isolation is the answer. What are some of the areas of healthy and life-giving sharing of the work of Christ in this world?

The cooperation between priests and sisters begins with grown-up models of the adult level. It begins with those who have achieved emotional maturity, not with those who are seeking it. This is the source of stability in any family, the soundness of the relationship between the adults. If this relationship is healthy, then the young will be healthy as well. They then have an example which influences them deeply and gives them a direction which is positive and trustworthy. Remove the adult figures, or, even worse, reveal them as mistrustful of each other, guarded and defensive, and the young will be confused and easily lost in their groping for growth.

There is immense, deeply Christian, and sacramental value in priests, brothers, and sisters of the Church learning to respect and work with each other for the sake of the Kingdom. However, without the example of respectful and restrained relationships on the part of mature priests and religious, the young ones may be yearning to work together, but there is just the chance that this work will not always be for the sake of the Kingdom. And, if we face our concerns, we are afraid that something like this could occur—and this is a realistic fear. But the Christian life is seeded with risk (although this is far different from rashness), and to back away from learning to love maturely is to indict Christianity itself.

The "God is dead" philosophy has a peculiar appeal to our students today, just as their perception of the advantages of personal fulfillment above all else does too. It is disturbing to find candidates, in a supposed life of faith, who are ready to question the sunrise itself. Perhaps a large measure of their bravado, their insistence on the primacy of the self, their readiness to mourn Divinity, flows from their own lack of sureness about themselves. But, in part, it may be because we priests and professed religious seem to them unsure of ourselves, somewhat mistrustful and timid, somewhat deadened to God.

If we are going to be the healthy mediators of development in the new generation, we must begin with ourselves and with the relationships between our most grown-up members. And mediators we must be because the young religious and seminarians need a great deal of understanding but also solid points of reference in the reality of adult figures who are secure in their vocations.

Areas of adult cooperation will be discussed in later chapters.

We must recognize that we are called to serve the People of God, we men and women, and the whole mystery of creation itself is mirrored in this. Perhaps we have more problems than we would have if we were able to work more of them out together, or at least to begin the process, or deepen it if it has already begun. If we are going to grow in the ministry of service to mankind, we are called, I think, to grow up together.

A century ago, Isaac Hecker spoke of the various solutions for the problems of the Church which would be presented by future generations. Some would see it in the liturgy, he predicted, and some in other movements. But the essential thing, the thing not attended to enough, and yet the very thing the Church would be most in need of, would be openness to the action of the Spirit. In an unparalleled way, this is the task for men and women in open and mature relationships within the Church.

"Woman," de Chardin tells us, "is put before man as the attraction and symbol of the world. Through woman, the universe advances to meet man." The same can be said for man as the source of opening the meaning of life for woman. This is preeminently true in the age in which we are found— in this age when the world thinks we can only play at life, when a great churchman fears that "no one will understand what we are trying to say." We can, as men and women given to God, reveal the richness of lives of faith, hope and real love; *Word* and *Spirit* working together to proclaim the good news to the very ends of the earth. Women are indeed called to be more than poor and, with the wealth of their womanhood, to enliven and to enrich the whole Church.

7/Sexuality and Emotional Maturity

THE discussion of sexuality in our day is something like the Fourth of July. It noisily celebrates freedom, inspires ponderous oratory, infects the young with excitement, and always draws a crowd. A steamy and clamorous holiday, it reaches its climax only after the evening star has set. The huddled spectators are momentarily thrilled and illumined by the arching rockets and the flags of fire falling in embers. And, as a kind breeze carries away the last shimmering but insubstantial tracery of light, the people go home, exhilaration yielding to weariness, pretty much the same as they have always been. But sex is more than fireworks just as freedom is more than a holiday. Brief and dazzling illumination is not enough for these large questions of life.

Sex has surely been the victim of an illusory independence of discussion. There has either been too much talk or far too little, too little feeling or an emotional excess. So we have also had too much data and too little wisdom, too many ideals and too few realisms, too much Puritanism, too much pornography, and perhaps too much poetry as well. Few observers have been able to get a clear view of sexuality in the human condition. Detached from humanity, sex has been trumpeted as the primal pulse of history or the fleeting failure of the flesh. Like the amateur psychotherapist, blindly delighting in diagnosis, who focuses so much on the symptom that he fails to find its root significance in the suffering person, we have so focused on sex that its larger meaning in man has been distorted and misunderstood.

Sexuality is hardly an appendage to the human personality. Man is sown with it. It flows through him, reflecting and expressing him. Sexuality is inescapably present in and will be a part of every person as long as he draws breath. Our understanding of it suffers quite as much when it is narrowly and animalistically exploited as when it is overromanticized or overspiritualized. When man reflects on himself he necessarily reflects on a sexual being.

What is it like, then, when an emotionally mature person turns his gaze inward? The fully grown are marked by a lack of fear of looking at themselves. They are open to all that they are, to the totality of their human experience. Defenses are down, and the mature can apprehend and accept their humanity, flawed though it may be, without undue uneasiness. No experience that arises within them need frighten them. This understanding encounter with the self is, in fact, fundamental to any integration and mature control of the self. If, as Harry Stack Sullivan has observed, "we are all more simply human than anything else," then a first sign of emotional growth is friendliness to ourselves as we are. Without this healthy love of himself, man can never be himself or give himself fully to anybody else. The sinner, St. Thomas reminds us, fails, not by loving himself too much but by failing to love himself enough.

And yet many men and women are relatively uncomfortable with themselves and consequently painfully uneasy with their sexuality. Ruled by a "tyranny of shoulds," they cannot accept what they are. They cannot forgive or love themselves in the human condition.

What is man that we are all so mindful of him? He is basically an imperfect, fallible, and growing organism. He makes mistakes, experiences a litany of assorted and often unbidden impulses; he can fall short but he can also measure up; he gets enthused but also bored; he has wide ideals and wild ideas all at the same time. A less than perfect piece, man finds that his troubles multiply when he ignores or forgets this. Man's maturity, the integration of all that he is, begins when he accepts and embraces fully his incarnation in the human family.

Sexuality is a healthy and positive dimension of personality that has broad expression in each man's words and work. This can surprise or dismay those who would wish sex away or those who insist that it constantly deliver for them unfailingly effulgent experiences. Genital sexuality has been employed variously as the proof of virility or femininity. Even the cold foregoing of it has been used at times by those who disdain humanity as a proof that they are thereby automatically sanctified. All of these attitudes are inhuman and immature.

Currently the trade in synthetic maturity plies manufactured man, the highly tooled automaton for whom sex is the sacrament of sophistication. The current folk hero is the man who can get ahead without giving, for whom loyalties are free of feeling and foundation, the sloe-eyed alien from the human condition who never loses his composure. The Commandments have been converted into an anemic code of competence. This hero, Bogart out of Hemingway by Warner Brothers, has made his own all of life's right moves. Never "losing his cool," he makes a knowledgeable and insulated passage through the world of men. He has mastered wine-lists, wenching, and cynical asides. He utters throwaway lines that say life really does not matter, that authority is for assaulting, that death is just the big sleep, and that the capital sin is really compassion. It is all deft capework on endless afternoons of hot sun and cool wine. The only sadness is that the matador gets old, or out of luck, and death courts him erotically into a dusty and lonely grave. Death seduces him away from the running of the bulls and the running of the sharks, and he finds himself impotent in its embrace.

The code of competence is enshrined in the celluloid scriptures of college film festivals where Bogart, in his curiously flickering immortality, makes the right moves and speaks the bright lines endlessly. But Bogart breathes no more and Bond has never breathed at all. The code of competence can only produce characters in search of personhood. It is all pursuit and never fulfillment and can never serve as a source of life and real love.

Love has a perishable place in these fictions. It is sexual capework, splendidly skilled passes that lead to animal conquering. It is so defensive, so overcontrolled and casual that one hardly notices the urgent pulse of these anxious heroes as they fruitlessly try to allay their hours of fear through repeated superficial moments of truth. Their synthetic, penultimate masculine enterprises are no substitute for authentic human experience. This rejection of maturity necessarily includes a rejection of mature sexuality. These muscular heroes are unable, in a final mockery of themselves, to enter the human condition at all. So turned in on themselves, they can never open themselves in a healthy way to anyone else. There is a feminine framework for this whole process too, unwarmed by the bright hues in which it is bathed by an armful of women's magazines. These are the failed men and women who are afraid of the dark and terribly afraid of the light as well. There is something almost unbearably sad about the aging playboys who think it is the height of manhood to nurse themselves at the breasts so bountifully proffered to them in the topless topography of the twentieth century. Bunny turns out to be a mother comforting and reassuring them that it is all right to be boys forever. The sadness lies, not in that anyone would call this sin, but that anyone would call this sophistication.

This cardboard cultural prototype for the "sexually liberated" male or female in reality places blinders on those fearful enough to fall for it. They live by pretentious defenses that block a full view of themselves and the reality that surrounds them. Just as restricted in their outlook, however, are those Christians who hold up a narrow view of overmystical sexuality, an intellectualized beatific vision of love at the summit. In this model, overidealized man and woman, as lifeless as the brooding plaster statues that used to oversee Times Square, propose a constant, concentrated, and incomparable Cana forever. Both these models confine themselves overmuch to genital sexuality. They demand that it deliver incredible glories successively and always more successfully. Frustration, disappointment, and self-doubt can easily arise from these approaches. In the first instance, the undeveloped men or women who pursue it find themselves plunged into the quicksand of their own adolescence. Their struggle does not free them but engulfs them deeper in their half-growth, and they can only claw and scratch blindly for personal survival. The second overintellectualized model fails in another way to face the human condition because it demands a divinized mystical experience in every union. This overfocus on genital sexuality demands what the human condition cannot possibly deliver.

Man gets tired and discouraged and is afflicted with myriad psychosomatic reactions. Man has good days and bad. The love that sustains him must have a broader base in his relationship to another than superbly successful genital union. It is not to make little of sexual intercourse to face the reality of its necessarily being interwoven with a richer pattern of fully shared life experiences. If we are successfully to open ourselves to our thorough sexuality, to our manhood and womanhood, we must necessarily open ourselves to the many levels, not all of them so smooth, of the human condition. Emotional maturity does not demand absolute perfection from a man, but it does demand the truth. This truth about our struggling, growing mysterious state still has the power to make us free.

To think we can be free of all contradictory, infantile, or frightening impulses, to deny their presence or their possibility, to fail to understand that fullness in the human condition may yet bear the vestiges of earlier stages of growth, to fly the pennant of technically successful orgasm as though this won the world series of life—all this is to demand of ourselves behavior that none of us can produce. To insist on an absolute in health or holiness that is beyond the relative possibilities of humanity at any given moment is to defeat ourselves. It is a lesson in how to fail at growing up by trying too hard. When we embrace the human condition realistically we allow ourselves room to grow, intellectually, emotionally, sexually, and in an harmonious and integrated fashion. We have learned, in a great lesson of the human condition, that Camelot never existed. But if Jacqueline Kennedy has emerged as less than Persephone, she is more of a person. Her character and dignity are deeper for being compounded with fierce feelings and less than perfect poise. We must open ourselves to the increasing consciousness we have of the fuller dimensions of human sexuality. We seem, strangely enough, very fond of spatial concepts in this regard. Bishop Robinson is uncomfortable with spatial parameters for God, and perhaps we should feel equally uncomfortable with them about man. We seek the *place* of sex in marriage. We draw lines within which to live and lines over which we are not to step. We set up directions, within and without, but these may be feeble hereditary modalities, as inappropriate for understanding man, as *up there* and *out there* are for understanding God. The emotionally mature man is charged with unsealing himself so that he may find and give all that he is in love. He must seek and uncover the sources of his defenses, so that he may be fully opened to the Spirit who will draw him more deeply into the life of the resurrection that is the calling of all Christians.

"Undivided love" has suffered, as a term, from the same territorial imperative that has made us so fond of spatial concepts. It conjures up a love given to God alone and a corollary fearsome reaming of the heart to eliminate all earthly attachments. Quite simply, however, undivided love means that genuine love, wherever and whenever it is found, is all of a piece. Real love everywhere is a share in the life of God, the presence of the Spirit of Love that is neither lessened nor divided no matter how many persons share in it. The great invitation to the emotionally mature, to those open to the action of the Spirit, is to surrender themselves, their sexuality, their manhood and womanhood, totally to his promptings. The Spirit of Love, once we share it, bids us to attain the full possibilities of our humanity. No man can foresee what these may be when he gives himself over to love. He can only respond by loving more, by bringing more of himself into being, by giving more fully in loving than he has ever been able to do before. The real crown of our overall maturity is in the response of our whole beings to the Spirit in the life of the Resurrection.

The Gospels, interestingly, speak not so often of man sinning or doing evil. They speak rather of men who are lost and who find themselves, not through fruitless posturing, but through opening themselves to God. This regularly occurs in the context of their relationship to their neighbor, in their openness to him in the whole range of human need. This is how the Spirit reaches us, through the way we let ourselves out as men and women to others. It is when we are closed to others, as the priest and levite were to the blood-covered man by the roadside, that we close ourselves off to the Spirit of Love.

In closing ourselves to the action of the Spirit, we have shut off the real source of our life, and all that is truly a part of our life. Emotionally mature sexuality, then, for the married or the celibate flows out of their fuller growth as persons in relationship to other persons under the guidance of the Spirit. This is the mystery of the resurrected life we lead. Only in a full acceptance of this life can our manhood or womanhood truly emerge. This is the challenge to our faith, to our healthy relevance and relatedness to the world of men. It is this faith that makes us whole.

We cannot, then, discuss sexuality or emotional maturity except in deeply human terms. It is through our humanity that the Spirit acts, and it is to a fullness of our humanity that the Spirit leads us. We do not expect this fullness to come overnight, because human growth is slow, demanding, and painful. But we sense that the unfolding of our total growth, including our sexuality, will lead us necessarily to a fuller giving of ourselves in love to others. It is unfortunate that so many contemporary discussions, such as those on birth control and celibacy, are carried on with minimal awareness of the painfully deep dimensions of love. Man must find all of himself, not just his sexuality or his rationality, if he would have the whole of himself to give to anyone. This is a lifelong process of yielding up the defenses that close us off from others and prevent the full growth of ourselves in relationship to them. Tillich's "courage to be" has rightly been completed by Jourard as "the courage to be known."

When this fundamental fact of life is grasped, men and women achieve their individuality as persons. They are not hounded by the cultural or philosophical prototypes of what *man* and *woman* should be. They are freed from trying to match themselves to an ill-fitting standard of the eternal masculine or feminine that is outside themselves. Quite unself-consciously they possess and express the fullness of all their authentic internal experience. The man will not be frightened to discover the gentler feminine elements in his personality, and the woman will be able to face, without apology, the strong and masculine elements within herself. They can be themselves, in the full confidence of their unique womanhood and manhood.

The great paradigm of growth is still found in the relationship of a full man and a full woman. In this rich relationship sexual union is a genuinely sublime sign of deep, personal love. But it is the personal love, something that invades all aspects of our being when we open ourselves to it, that informs the sexual relationship. The personal relationship does not have its origin, although it finds nourishment, in the sexual act. It finds nourishment, however, in the whole range of marital interactions. It can be profound even in absence and in separation, even in the sacrifice of the sexual act at times.

This implies that the great sharing, the communion

yearned for so deeply by those who are genuinely led by the Spirit of Love, is never complete, that fulfillment is never final, that the essence of the experience, even in the highest order of human love, can only find the lovers urgently longing for a deeper and more permanent oneness. True lovers could wish their bones and flesh, the unyielding boundaries of their selfhood, to crumble and dissolve, so that their gift and surrender might be quietly and finally complete. But in the human condition, even this deepest of longings is impossible. If there is a little death in the gift of themselves to each other, lovers find yet another death in their inability to commingle totally their persons. They suffer this death and they are resurrected through the expanded love that is theirs. Through this counterpoint of dying and rising their mutual love is fed heartily and they are redeemed.

This love of great caring and trust, this communion, gently opens out into newer and deeper dimensions that they must enter in faith. And here they find that their giving, their living and dying, is never done. Man and woman who love like this are constantly challenged to grow, one yielding the self to the other even as the other gives more of the self to him. So love is never summed up or totally and fully expressed through the sharing of their bodies. It is the wholeness of their persons, the never ending treasures of all that they are, breath, blood, and spirit, that they yearn to blend together with such painful intensity that life itself is not time enough for the task.

This deep love, the life of the Spirit, provides the only real insight we have into God who would share his life eternally with us. It challenges a man and a woman to realize the wholeness of their womanhood and manhood in relationship to one another. They are led to a communion in God that transcends, although it does not belittle, their healthy and truly holy genital relationship. For them heaven will not be a rude shock or a surprise. They will find that they have already known something of the inexhaustible riches of their eternal union in God himself. The resurrected life of their marriage will only open them further and yet find them completely filled in the eternal moment of heaven.

This goal is one that inevitably is presented to those earnestly opening themselves to the action of the Spirit of Love in this life. It is in no way a lessening of the importance of genital sexuality to grasp the frightening realism of the Christian's vocation in marriage to love ever more totally and ever more fully with all of his humanity. It is no fragrant scented angelism to understand that life in the Spirit can only beckon us out of ourselves at every instant. That is why St. Paul makes so much of the utter freedom from law that is the sign of those given over to the life of the Spirit. The world of the Spirit has never been mapped or charted. That is why categories, manuals, and all the good advice of all the wise men who have gone before us are of no account. Lovers find their way together when they open themselves, without defenses, to God's action in them.

The great task for those in love is not to get information that will prepare them for well-performed sexual acts but to discover within themselves the obstacles that prevent their full surrender to the life of the Spirit. It is in this relationship of deepening mutual trust that defenses peel away because they are no longer needed. The feast of life is fitting when man who was lost is found, when man who was dead comes to life in love. This is Christian realism about emotional maturity and sexuality. Maturity means full growth, the full understanding and love of ourselves, that frees us to give our whole selves ever more fully in love. Love that is genuine, we are told, will outlast prophecies, but its flames are searing. This is the kind of love that stokes the furnaces of the universe, the love we cannot grasp, but the love that can never be lost either, once we have given ourselves over to it.

St. Thomas long ago suggested that man loves on three levels, the animal level, the level of sense, and, ultimately and appropriately, on the level of the inner self. The animal level, instinctive and snarlingly self-preserving, is familiar to all. The next plane, that of man's senses, is higher still but not the highest of possibilities for man. Here he satisfies the senses, and he has a whole world full of wonders, sensible, possessable, clutchable, that reward him. The highest challenge is the love of the true inner self. This is the rightful love of self that makes it possible for him to be a person at all.

It is to this level that we are all called. A fully integrated sexuality is found only in those who have some feeling for the breathtaking demands on their total selves that life-giving love demands. Only when this is understood can the genital expression of sexuality in marriage or the sacrifice of it in celibacy be comprehended or lived with any kind of meaning. Only when fully grown men face all the facts, can they bring any wisdom to the great questions about sex that worry us. Only at this level will men who are lost find themselves and the fullness of life that is theirs in redemptive sharing. This is the perspective in which we must view ourselves; this is the challenge we must steel ourselves to accept; this is the whole of it for all of us struggling to do our best in the human condition. If "life", as Abigail Adams wrote, "is for those who love" then this is the fullness of life in which is found the fullness of emotional and sexual maturity, promised, as the fruit of the Spirit, for all Christians.

8 / Celibacy:
Clamors and Quiet Questions

CELIBACY, as has been noted often in these pages, has been the subject of a great deal of intense but often superficial discussion. To point this out does not mean that one feels that the discussion should be stopped. Indeed, it must be deepened. There is no way effectively to shut off questions that gnaw at the heart of man. When an individual tries to solve problems by suppressing them, it simply does not work. They reappear, none of their squirming energy lost, in disguised forms. The Church does not succeed with suppression any better than the individual. Under an assumed name the problem gets a passport back to consciousness.

Pope Paul VI has been charged with just such a maneuver in forbidding the discussion of celibacy before the tiers of applauding prelates at Vatican II. This is, however, an unfair accusation. No one probably senses more keenly than he the need to reexamine the question of clerical celibacy. And yet no one sees as clearly as he how unprepared the Church is for a mature discussion of this question at the present time. Before it can be discussed, the ideal of celibacy must be refurbished and reidentified. The issue must be examined in the light of genuine comprehension of the meaning of life and love. The Church, just like any person examining an issue in relationship to himself, must be fully informed about both.

The ideal of celibacy must first be perceived as a gift of the Spirit. Given the nature of gifts, it cannot be presumed that it is given to everyone. If some understanding of the human person must inform all discussions concerning the Church, it is necessary to localize the gift to the inner life of an individual rather than to the corporate behavior of a class of individuals. The response must be as free as the gift. Otherwise the whole meaning of gift and free response are destroyed. In the same way, celibacy, or any other gift, can only be distorted and demeaned if it is not seen in the context of the uncategorizable mysteries of God's relationship to man. When the system that ignores the nature of a gift does not work, the temptation is to deny the meaning of the gift itself.

In point of fact, celibacy challenges a man to the very nub of his being, not just to give up marriage, but to surrender himself totally to the action of the Spirit. The challenge for the married man is equally deep, but the marriage relationship itself is a massive immediate source of interpersonal support. We have observed that the invitation offered to the celibate or the married Christian is fundamentally the same. They must give of themselves in love that is real and unrelenting in its demands on their persons.

First of all, celibacy is not a necessarily abnormal state. Many have denied the possibilities of a life in which the sexual expression of marriage could be successfully sacrificed. Only harm could come to the individual who would try a life like that. Aside from the fact, often confided to marriage counselors, that deeply loving husbands and wives often express their most unselfish affection for the other by foregoing sexual relations at times out of consideration for the health or other needs of their partner, modern day experts do not fully agree with this diagnosis. Marriage and maturity are made of more than genital sexual relationships. Dr. Mary Calderone, well-known specialist in the field of sex education, recently declared: "Indeed, it is essential also to understand that those who are voluntarily celibate are not all, or should not be, 'asexual' beings, . . . If they have come to terms with their sexuality in ways other than regressive fashion, they will be able to deal with those who come under their care warmly and creatively. I have known nuns and priests who, in this way, were more truly sexual beings in the broadest sense of the term, than married people I have known."

As noted in a previous chapter, the arguments supporting the celibate state of the priest have not always been quite as convincing, or as fair to noncelibates, as they might be.

Perhaps, aside from faith, no argument or explanation can make sense of celibate lives. The most helpful arguments, however, are grounded in some grasp of what genuine human love is all about. Priests are supposed to help men understand God and his message for them. They have the task of translating God into terms that can mean something to his creatures. The only way we get any satisfying idea of God is through realizing what is highest and best in man himself. Only men who understand the experience of really loving someone and the wish to share one's life with the beloved can understand the God who is described as loving us and wanting to share his life with us.

Seen with the eyes of faith, celibacy is a gift of God that fits the way men are made and enables certain men and women to give all they are and have in the service of others. No man can possibly carry out his mission in the priesthood without being able to love, not just as the sentimental good guy of a hundred bad movies, but as a strong person who is ready to pay the price of dying in order that others may live. Only when he genuinely and thoroughly lives the sacrificial life of Jesus Christ can the priest take Christ's place in the lives of modern men. Men will not accept faith except from men who live by faith, and the sacrifices of celibacy are a clear sign of the strength of the priest's own faith.

Can this troubled world use an example of lovers who are this strong? Can the clergy themselves, whose misadventures in trying to persuade men through power plays are already too well chronicled, accept an ideal that demands so much?

Human lives dominated by loving faith may be the last best chance of redeeming religion from its widely proclaimed irrelevance. It is not that there has been too much celibacy for the tastes of the world. It is that there has been too little sacrificial celibacy witnessed in the world.

The celibate priest or religious man or woman who understands his life is trying to live as his Master, Christ, did. They are not afraid of the world or marriage. They must, to understand the measure of their celibacy, love a great deal to give up the woman or the man they could love magnificently. This is the only kind of person fit to respond to the gift of celibacy —the kind of man who knows what life with a woman who would be the mother of his children could be like; the kind of woman who understands how deeply she would give herself to the man who would be the father of her children. There is no other way for any man or woman summoned to grow up and to learn to love others truly and deeply.

Celibacy cannot be understood solely in terms of restraint or abstention from relationships with members of the other sex. It can be a worthy ideal only when it is seen in the context of the man-woman dimensions of the Church. It is a fully realized ideal only in the lives of those who can move in the reality of the dynamics of the Church's life. Celibacy has no life at all when it is just a bachelor's burden or the lightly defended integrity of the aloof virgin. It means something when men and women who realize the values of life and of each other live it fully.

In the light of much recent speculation, especially over the decisions of great figures to leave the Church and to marry, we must consider not only the possibility but the presence of celibate love within the Church. The discussion of this is necessary, first of all, because of the need of all men and women for the experience of genuine love, and, secondly, because it is an observable reality. No question of the meaning of celibacy as a gift of the Spirit made to be operative in a human context is complete without it.

The Catholic world reacted strongly when Father Charles Davis withdrew from the Church just before Christmas in 1966. The reaction was deep because here was a man who had been a mediator, an understanding interpreter of the Church's struggle for renewal. Here he was saying in effect to the world, "No, it is no use. Not within the institutional Church." And he struck at the very underpinnings of the hopes of many Catholics.

He underscored this in his first statement to the press which read in part: "I am marrying to rebuild my life on personal love I can recognize as true and real after a life surrounded in the Church by so much that at best is irrelevant and at worst an obstacle to genuine human experience. I am still a Christian, but I reject the institution of the Church." Father Davis' fellow Christians reacted with understanding that was deep and genuine. In great numbers they wondered whether he felt very alone in grappling with the elements of his decision. They could only gather from his phrases, filled with feeling, that he perceived the institutional Church as incapable of being either the source or the instrument of the deep sharing of personal love. He seemed to say that the Mystical Body had become hopelessly arthritic under the burdens of the organized Church and, so, unable to embrace humanity in any genuine way.

Charles Davis highlighted the aching heart of renewal itself, the gigantic and painful effort of Christians to love the world deeply and truly. His move out of the Church crystallized the situation of thousands of priests and religious who found themselves confronting the contradiction of seemingly loveless structures that go by grand but empty names. These men and women had come to understand the reformers in their hearts much better than they ever had with their minds alone. However, they did not and do not reject the core meaning of incarnation. If anything, these priests, religious, and laity typified the Christians who are beginning to grasp the weight of taking on the human condition, with all it terrors and challenges, as they never dreamed of before.

In the very midst of the questioning of celibacy which was intensified by Father Davis' decision, a deep realization of the challenge to human love for the servants of the Church has come into being. The fact is that many priests and religious have found great human love in their lives. It has come unsought and unexplained, as real love often does, and it has borne all the signs of the action of the Spirit within them. They find themselves quite uncomforted by the manuals and strictures about earthly attachments obscuring eternal goals. Unverbalized, unwritten about, the presence of genuine loving relationships can be observed in the lives of priests and religious throughout the land. The concrete truth is that these servants of the Church have experienced deep human love and it has seemed to them a realization rather than a contradiction of their vocations. They have found this love within the very structures in which Father Davis lost faith.

An agony of growth is occuring within these priests and religious who have felt their own true depths sounded by the unbidden entrance of real love into their lives. They have found a love that brings them to life, that brings its gifts of pain and peace at the same time. For the first time, in the experience of trusting and being trusted by another person, they have had to confront their celibacy with a heightened faith. But in opening themselves to this love, they have discovered a freedom and energy to understand and love the world that was never provided by all their so-called practices of perfection. It is as though the Spirit would humanize them as individuals as the only valid starting point in humanizing the earthly organization of the Church. As they see it, they cannot reject this gift of love that has transformed their lives and given them the courage and strength of completed personhood. Neither do they understand it fully nor know what it will demand of them or where it will lead them. This has developed as one of the clearest, yet most quiet, of current Catholic questions.

These are the Christians who understand that the Incarnation must take place in them. They realize that it demands real relationships within the human family and that if these occur, relevancy will inevitably follow. An unparalleled and unpublicized Pentecost has occurred, not so much through institutions as through individuals. These signs of the surging of the Spirit have been found in every diocese, every community, among the laity as well as priests and religious. As one who has listened and talked to dozens of these apostles who feel deep human love in their lives, I can only identify it as healthy. It is not sentimentality nor a slightly retarded adolescent ardor. As I have seen it lighting up the lives of priests, brothers, sisters, and those whom they serve, it is the deeply wonderful and deeply realistic sharing and sacrificing of each other that is genuine love. Unlike absorbing and self-satisfying crushes or particular friendships, these relationships do not distract people from their work. They seem, on the other hand, to enable them to serve more fully, with a greater giving of themselves to those to whom they minister or teach.

These relationships are not fantastic voyages into a land that does not exist. They bring the individuals who experience them into the workaday world, into the heart of mankind itself, with an unretouched view of the human condition and its crying needs. These men and women, signed with the cross of religious profession, are facing themselves, the whole undefended gamut of their deepest personal feelings, not to surrender in self-delusion to them, but with a deepened willingness to give all of themselves in great fullness to others.

They experience their deepened sense of incarnation in relationship to mankind, not as a splendid ascetic escape, but as a pain-ridden pilgrimage in which nothing that is human is alien to them. They must understand more deeply their vows of celibacy, because in the inspiriting encounter of full man and full woman they can afford nothing less than fully realized commitment to these vows. They are as unimpressed by the unrealistic and inhuman arguments often presented for celibacy as they are by the archly uninformed arguments frequently proposed against it. They have found that there is in the life of the Spirit a freedom of relationship coupled with a sacrificial demand that leads to a deeper union and a more complete offering than was ever sketched out for them in the failed blueprints of another time. Their celibacy is a great singing sign of total giving to the People of God, to the many for whom Christ died. Agreeing with the truism that sex without love is a sin, they understand even more clearly that celibacy without love is also a sin. These men and women are, it seems to me, the wise virgins who have discovered treasures of energy of their own. They light up the world's darkness with the flames of the Spirit burning within themselves.

There are, I also know from experience, foolish virgins as well, those with no oil of their own who can only clamor noisily in the night for fuel they have never earned. Largely narcissistic, they confuse posturing with a passion for life. They insist on instant intimacy, a kindergarten Christianity that can only play house with adult Christian values. It speaks but never really understands the language of personalism. They are hardly to be despised but neither are they to be imitated. Theirs is a ghostly Christianity, a cloying, spun sugar view of life in which the wedding reception never ends and the reality of human relationships never begins. But, as the action of the Spirit is inevitable to those opening themselves to it, so they will one day face the rigors of growing up.

Where are we then? The structures of priestly and religious life leave little room for the conscious expression of healthy and holy love in the Spirit between consecrated men and women. By "conscious expression" I mean the simple opportunities for correspondence, for visits, or even for working together. Some aspects of the Church's institutional structures have apparently been built on a suspicion of even the most open and healthy kinds of sharing by the men and women of the Church. This is a strange contradiction to the Incarnation which began in the setting of the celibate sacrificial love of Mary and Joseph. Christ himself was not ill at ease in his many deep relationships with his friends. The new Gospel translations underscore his openness by the vigorous language used to describe his attitude toward others. For example, we read that he "really loved" Martha, Mary, and Lazarus. He constantly expressed his human feelings quite openly. He mourned his friend, he wept over Jerusalem, and it is difficult to believe that his love for others was anything different from what we experience in the deepest human love.

Wipe out celibacy and the problem of human love still remains. Is this the penultimate age, when we urgently must read the signs of the times? The Spirit is obviously at work, seeding the world with rich relationships that can never become fruitful by the approved but archaic husbandry of the past. Something wonderfully human has entered the Church, has burgeoned without corporate cultivation, something that puts self-conscious Catholics and their crying on the night streets for someone else's oil into perspective.

This kind of love seems to be a gift of the Spirit and it cannot be demanded or actively sought. There is, as with all gifts, a mystery involved in why it should be given to some and not to others, or why in fact it is given at all. There are many servants in the Church, in all the ranks of its membership, who have not experienced this gift. This makes them in no way less dedicated. They give of themselves, and their lives are also signs of living faith.

The large questions are concerned with whether the institutional Church can make room for healthy celibate love, whether it can dare to believe that what it proclaims about the action of the Spirit in the hearts of men is indeed true. Obviously, the structures of the Church must be transformed in view of the fire that has been kindled on the face of the earth. There is little time, perhaps none at all, to muster a reassuring restoration of life as it once was. There is no patience for renewal that is reducible, after the model of the airlines and railroads, to revisions of a daily schedule. All time is run out, a horned and outworn skin has been moulted. Nobody will ever believe again that his offering of self to the redemption of the world entails a suicidal destruction of that self at the same time.

There is no subject more delicate and surely none that is more patient of misunderstanding than this. The immature quickly appropriate reflections like these to their own ends and to satisfy their own needs. There is no way to prevent this without penalizing the healthy and mature who understand the values and responsibilities of human relationships. These mature Christians understand the struggles that Charles Davis seemingly underwent. Opening themselves earnestly to the Spirit in the same searching of themselves, they have answered with an affirmation rather than a rejection of the Church. In their faith and openness genuine hope for renewal from within is clearly revealed.

It is true that this great dimension of life in the Spirit has not been unknown in the history of the Church. It is undeniably true, however, that a conscious facing up to the issue has come only in postconciliar times. The problems underlying the great questions of birth control and celibacy cannot be grasped unless the limitless possibilities of the action of the Spirit of Love are acknowledged. It is not quite so simple as changing a few laws and thereby guaranteeing the happiness of married couples or of priests and religious. The whole vision of Christian life suggests that the underlying problem of love between persons must first be plumbed as deeply as possible. This seemed to be clearly part of de Chardin's epic reflections on evolving man. And so he could write:

No matter how primordial and structural as may be the fulfilling encounter of the sexes, we have no proof that we as yet possess an exact idea of the best functioning and forms of this fundamental complementarity. Marriage is socially polarized on the basis of personal fulfillment and reproduction, whereas religious perfection, theologically, is presented in terms of separation. We decidedly need a *third* way. Not flight by withdrawal but conquest by sublimation of the profound powers dormant under the mutual attraction of the two sexes . . . Such is, I am more and more persuaded, chastity's secret essence and magnificent task.

And, in another place he would pursue the same line of thought:

Some day, after mastering the winds, the waves, the tides, and gravity, we shall harness, for God, the energies of love. And then, for the second time in the history of the world, man will have discovered fire.

If, as Andrew Greeley has observed, we lack but urgently need a theology of celibacy, it may well have to follow de Chardin's thought. It surely must come to terms with the valid witness of loving celibate lives. If man, under the action of the Spirit, is to become all that his destiny seems to promise, then he must learn to give and share all that he is in the most profound way possible. No aspect of his potential can be left unexplored if man's great voyage to fullness is to be accomplished.

Only a very naive person would presume that the implications of these themes are fully grasped today. It would take an equally naive person to ignore the obvious difficulties and dangers of making room for human love of this order in the lives of priests, religious, and the apostolic laity. It is helpful, insofar as our limited observation and understanding allow, to describe further some of the characteristics of healthy celibate love.

First of all, there is a deep consciousness that this transcendent gift of the Spirit is never given just for the fulfillment of the individuals who experience it. It seems, in fact, that they must be prepared for this kind of relationship by first attaining a certain level of maturity. They must, in other words, already have given themselves to God earnestly and unconditionally. A hard won openness to the Spirit through a surrender of themselves seems to be a necessary predisposition to the gift which we have, howsoever incompletely, described. It is not a gift to be demanded or grabbed at by anybody at any stage of his or her growth or development.

Secondly, it is neither a reward for good uncomplaining behavior nor a prize to be clutched to the breast of those who seek it. When this gift is given, it is not for any individual or pair of individuals. It is given for the sake of the Church, to enable apostles to serve the People of God more fully. This profoundly challenging invitation to live by the Spirit in an uncompromisingly generous way is never given for purely personal fulfillment. It is not something any one can call "mine." In every sense, it must be referred to by those giving their lives to others through the Church as "ours."

Thirdly, it is not just a means of growth, enlightenment, or enjoyment for those who are asked to respond to it. A person will undoubtedly grow and be enlightened in and through such deep respectful love. This love, when it is the work of the Spirit, cannot rest within the persons who experience it. They must share it, unafraid of losing it, with all those with whom they come in contact. The whole meaning of this gift of love is to develop fully the manhood and womanhood of the Church's servants so that their gift of themselves to the People of God will be as total and as effective as possible.

This brings us back to the psychological necessity of priests and religious possessing the fullness of themselves, of their masculinity and femininity, if their apostolate is to be healthy. This is also necessary for the fullness of the Church as the People of God. Only if lives of service to the Church not only offer but demand the complete gift of manhood and womanhood, will they be deeply attractive to the healthiest personalities. Too many versions of priestly and religious life have seemed in the past to put a premium on a neutral quality of personhood. The hero and the potential saint have been presented as the man or woman who needed no other person in this world. All nice and neat and inhuman.

The only persons who can attain the fullness of holiness, the full presence of the Spirit within them, are those who can attain the fullness of their humanity. If the Church has a deep need at the present moment, it is for personalities that are rich and deep in their manhood and womanhood. These are not only the healthy ones who bring life to the full to the People of God, they are also the ones who are alone capable of embracing a living celibacy. Their chastity is the vital sign of men and women who can face and accept the invitation by the Spirit to give of themselves completely for the sake of the People of God.

Unless the apostolate clearly challenges the complete realization of a person's thorough personality, there can only be the unfortunate multiplication of the pseudo vocations of incomplete persons. It is no secret that the priesthood and religious life have seemed sexless preserves and have, therefore, attracted many applicants whose strong internal needs were met and satisfied by such an environment. All too often, despite the pain we must suffer to make it public, there has been a sanctification and subsidization of half-grown or distorted persons within the priesthood and religious life.

There has been an appeal to what could only be described as the homosexual virgin. This type of person gravitates to a life that de-emphasizes not only marriage but even the desirability of any kind of deep relationship with the opposite sex. The homosexual character type, by no means necessarily an overt homosexual in behavior, is comfortable in a life that absolves him and rewards him for rejecting a heterosexual environment. The homosexual character type may, in fact, exhibit superficially splendid behavior, especially during a period of training. Celibacy and the vow of chastity, always presented to him in terms of relationships with the other sex, are not great challenges to him. He can move forward on the glossy but dangerously thin surface of life. It may take a close eye to detect the subtle dynamics of his true character at work. The homosexual virgin prizes power and sets out to acquire it with a polished indirection that is just this side of deviousness. The homosexual virgin deals in anything but a straightforward manner with others. In most cases, he is divisive but also quite successful in attaining influential positions. He is terribly threatened by fully grown men and women and frequently manages to make these latter suffer a good deal.

The homosexual virgin is incapable of living a life of celibacy that is a sign of anything but selfishness. It is a far greater sorrow that the priesthood and religious life should be attractive to these people than it is that it could possibly make room for men and women capable of loving one another. There is a hideous hypocrisy that must be faced about the acceptability of half-persons whose decorous and dead behavior never raises the problems that celibate love does. There is something sodden about any structure that can support the sick because they seem to present an acceptable facade, especially in the area of heterosexual relationships.

There is just not enough life in these people, not enough fullness or individuality, to enable them to share much that is richly human with the People of God. Propriety is not yet the soundest foundation for the development of the priesthood or religious life.

The Church deserves servants more capable of growth to sustain and serve it in this world. It must open itself to its men and women so that they can open themselves to their own manhood and womanhood. Only in fullness of selfhood can men and women reach beyond themselves and live for the sake of the Church. No celibacy or chastity will move the world unless it is embraced and lived sacrificially by thoroughly developed men and women. The great mystery of God's redemptive work in this world is made manifest only through the men and women who live and love fully enough to touch and open the heart of modern men to the action of the Spirit. The Gospels ask the question as to whether Christ, when he comes again, will find faith on the earth. The answer will be *yes* only if the humanity of the Church's servants has been completely opened to the action of the Spirit.

9/Health and Holiness in the Church

THE Gospels sing of healthy things, of fish and bread and salt, of life and light and real love. There is nothing self-conscious about these pages that tell us of the conditions of life in Christ. The men and women who serve the Church need a basic soundness of personality to live their vocations fully. Normal and healthy people alone can respond whole-heartedly to the promptings of the Spirit. This is so because only the normal person is conscious enough of his own needs not to be mastered by them. Only the open and strong person can possess himself fully enough to give himself freely to others.

Where there is excessive inner psychological need, or a marked distortion or stunting of the basic character structure, the individual becomes trapped in an intrapersonal morass. The man or woman thus entangled tends to invest available energies in unraveling the self, and has little to employ freely in serving others. Those incapable of reaching maturity because of personal psychological difficulties have a merited claim on our sympathies, but their place is not in the active apostolate. This is not to judge these people harshly but to apply the lessons of experience, research, and reflection to the question of the qualifications of the servants of the People of God. It is to recognize, in the light of the main thesis of this book, that freedom from major emotional impediments is necessary if fully developed men and women in relationship to each other in the apostolate are to provide the only viable model for the structures of a new age.

Men and women can never work successfully together for the sake of the Church if their inner needs force them to lesser levels of relationships that are more truly for the sake of themselves. Healthy people find life a struggle. They have, however, the resources to achieve their fullness through the very process of struggle that characterizes growth. These same healthy people will be free from self-seeking at certain stages in their development. They possess the fundamental soundness to pass through these stages and to continue to grow, as they must throughout their life, toward greater self-lessness. Basically healthy people have, in brief, the capacity for maturity that the psychologically impoverished do not possess.

It is worth observing that in many listings of the characteristics of healthy people, the quality of openness is always at or near the top. This term, or some rough equivalent, expresses the kind of person who is open to himself and all that he is. Defensiveness is not a major mode of adjustment and so the mature person can be open to other persons quite freely as well. This quality of being open, highly prized and easily recognized by all men, is also absolutely necessary if the Holy Spirit is to work in and through the person. The Spirit is not a supernatural laser beam that dissolves psychological blocks and defenses. Major psychological obstacles within the person have a hideous strength in that they can frustrate the action of the Spirit. The men and women who must live by the Spirit cannot, in fact, do this if they are not relatively integrated as persons and therefore open to his promptings.

Any number of examples could be given in illustration of this point. The homosexual person referred to in the previous chapter is a case in point. Homosexual character types are not just like healthy people except for a variant sexual appetite. They are, insofar as we can understand them, related to themselves and to others in a basically distorted way. It is not to condemn them but to save them from grief that we must exclude them from a calling that demands full manhood or womanhood. Too many grievous problems have arisen both for the individuals and the institutions of the Church because these afflicted people have been attracted by certain aspects of the priesthood or religious life. If their celibacy is in a sense proper, it is also unproductive. There is a terrible barren quality about these persons that comes through in their ministry or teaching. It is true that they have often been more sinned against than sinning, and that they have frequently been motivated by subconscious forces that they themselves do not understand. This makes it no less imperative to rule them out as candidates for the ranks of the priesthood or religious life.

This is also true of the startlingly undeveloped personalities who are attracted to a life, the styles of which at times have allowed them to be supported and sustained by a regime that makes all the decisions for them. To be dominated is, for them, to stay alive. This is not good enough at a time when the needs of the Church demand strong and self-determining personalities.

The same could be said of the obsessive-compulsive personalities whose response is to some distant and demanding Divinity. Driven on by internal needs, for behavior that is somehow "perfect" and controlled, they give themselves out of fear to structures that relieve their anxiety by rigid and often highly neurotic rules of life. An endless need to be approved and to be at ease with ill-developed consciences attracts them into elaborately codified lives. A free response to the Spirit of Love is impossible to these individuals who are so unfortunately trapped in the strangling inner strands of their own needs.

The massive shifts now irreversibly underway within the Church are all away from excessive control and towards greater personal freedom for priests and religious. Some may argue this point but, in the face of what is occurring in a Church that has placed itself fully on the side of human freedom, they will never be able to refute it. The weak and inadequate have been among the first to suffer in the atmosphere of aggiornamento because it is stripping them of the defenses that made certain forms of service to the Church appealing to them in the first place. Their whole world falls apart because they fall apart when controls are withdrawn. These are the people not strong enough or sure enough of their own identification to live free, adult Christian lives. The defections of postconciliar times are not just a debacle. They are frequently the signs of individuals who are too weak to live a life that is not carefully and constantly supervised. Two things stand out in regard to this:

(1) Unhealthy people whose inadequacy or pathology was previously masked by rigid control in institutionalized living are disintegrating in an atmosphere of freedom, trust, and uncertainty.

(2) Healthy individuals are undergoing severe trials in groups or dioceses or seminaries where the atmosphere has not been affected by Vatican II and its renewed vision of the Church.

Because things have remained unchanged, the unhealthy hang on, but many of the healthy, in great pain and regret, are looking for other vocational opportunities within the Church.

This whole area is important because it is clear that the role of the full woman and the full man in the Church cannot be filled by someone who is not or never can be a full woman or man. Unfortunately, this latter type is all too easy to come by these days, and in the absence of the numbers that are needed for the apostolate, superiors can be tempted to compromise. But this is an area where compromise is neither feasible nor prudent. A great many people in formation work are uneasy because so many young men and women are leaving training houses these days, but it is possible that they have the problem just backwards. Others are uneasy, not because too many are leaving, but because too few are leaving. This is a genuine part of the problem today: to be strong enough and to possess vision enough to understand that the more realistic conditions of our lives (change, uncertainty, etc.) are unveiling the inadequate for what they are. By all means, let them leave. Only when the renewed religious life emerges, as it surely must, as a life for grown-up people, will the vocational problem be alleviated. For it is renewed religious life, a challenge to the fit rather than the faltering, which will make it possible for the Spirit to reach a new generation of better candidates for the Church.

In line with this, many are also appalled by the serious kinds of problems that are found among candidates in late stages of training these days. This is a result of the same phenomenon. The less rigid the situation of control, the earlier will latent problems manifest themselves, and, as a result, we have candidates who are experiencing serious difficulties before ordination or profession whereas in a previous era the problems would only have appeared later on. This is not a disaster but a distinct advantage for all concerned. The worst thing we could do would be to fail to understand what these outbreaks of difficulties, often in the interpersonal areas, really mean. It is fruitless to invest healthy energy in patching up these people in some naive hope that all will go well later on. Those in formation work need the grace-guided strength to let them go, to a better world by far, because it will be the best thing for them and, despite the difficulties, the best thing for their religious communities as well.

This is not the time to lower requirements but to increase them. Nor is it the time to try to accommodate training programs for the weak, but rather to make them mature enough for the strong. Religious communities are supposed to be homes, not psychiatric hospitals; but the difference is sometimes difficult to discern. If the present age is pressing on us the unavoidable anxieties of normal, healthy living, then we must seek and admit only those candidates who can, within human limits, live this way. Service to the Church through the priesthood and religious life is meant to be an expression of the human persons drawn to it by grace, not a solution for the deep problems of the disturbed human persons drawn into it by disorder. I am not trying to sketch an ideal that is unapprochable by the average candidate, because, after all, all life is meant to be characterized by growth. I do want to emphasize that greater care than ever is needed in the selection of candidates. The religious life is a place for people to be healthy but, for too many, it becomes a place to be ill. These considerations are all the more important at a time when the form of religious life is evolving and when strong and healthy people, even in diminished numbers, will be needed as never before.

The strong need encouragement more than control; they must be freed, insofar as possible, from the burden of spending most of their time and effort comforting or covering up for their inadequate companions in religious life. For, with the emphasis always on what is normal and healthy, the future of religious life depends on them. The Church's men and women are called to be more than poor. They must be rich in the real stuff of life.

We might as well get accustomed to the idea that the forms of religious life are indeed evolving, and that is basically a healthy thing. Only healthy persons can oversee this growth and only healthy persons will be able to live it, because it will be rooted in more genuine freedom, not just in altered schedules of exercises or procedures. It will demand more of the hard-to-give qualities of trust, not the chaos of children abandoned by their elders. It will demand more real love, not just the yearning for it or the suppression of it because of fear. In other words, priests and religious will have to live in the human family if they are going to live at all. This is the time for enlarged hearts to match the enlarged sense of values which must guide us into this new age. It will be full of pain and problems, but after all life is not meant to be pain- or problem-free.

There are subtler forms of personal disorder that have come to the surface in this age of personalistic emphasis. They are even more dangerous for the Church because these people fancy themselves as the proponents of freedom, love, and all the good things celebrated by true Christianity. A strong strain of sickness runs through this half-grown group. Most characteristic of them is that they sing their songs of freedom, love, and sharing chiefly for themselves. They are altogether too self-conscious in the claims they make on each other. Affectation and superficiality, no matter how beautifully interwoven these are with the phrases of personalism, are the hallmark of their behavior. They feast on rather than feed the People of God. All too often, in the dreadfully "in" world they create, innocent people are hurt, some permanently. They may speak of a sacrificial celibate love but they practice a self-satisfying perversion of it. They actively seek intimacy and advocate "therapeutic affection" and other practices that are overlain with a fine patina of latent homosexuality. They may indeed deserve our sympathy and loving understanding but in no way our admiration or imitation. We can do without these unhealthy allies in the cause of Christianity. It is time we rooted out this evil that grows like wildly multiplying cancer cells in the Mystical Body.

In the long run only health is reliable. The great growth of the People of God must be rooted in what is right and sound about its men and women. Otherwise, the human relationships that must be the basis for the future structures of the Church will be seriously faulted. The action of the Spirit will be blunted by anything less than an insistence on the fullness of manhood and womanhood that alone can bring life to the full to the Church.

To adopt this scale of values one may have to settle for fewer priests and religious. This is not necessarily a problem, especially in view of the anticipated increased participation of all the People of God in works formerly reserved for the clergy and professed religious. Fewer numbers may indeed be a blessing, especially if the purity and intensity of the Church's servants constitute a clearer sign of the Spirit's action in the world.

One of the marks of the People of God is holiness, and the word holy comes from an old English word that means "healthy." The great mark of holiness will be manifested to the world only through men and women who have first achieved their own wholeness. It takes healthy men and women to love their enemies, to give all of themselves to others, and to heal the wounds of the human race.

III/FORMS FOR THE FUTURE

10 / Values for the Future

A MEASURE of the pain and frustration of many members of today's Catholic community is their realization of how seminary-innocent they have been for so long about so many truths of life. Like the people of Florence, so sure the rivers would never rise that they scattered their treasures in their cellars, these Catholics cannot forgive themselves for the faith they gave so unquestioningly to structures and categories that have now proved flimsy and incapable of giving either protection or comfort.

One of the fascinating things about men after a disaster is their unwillingness to believe that it will happen again. So the sodden Italian canvases and folios, now drying in the sun, may be stored once more below the waterline. People tend to settle again by a sea that has boiled over them or in the shadow of mountains that have shuddered and fallen on them. They find it reassuring to get back to the decent and distracting details of life and to leave unsolved the more fundamental problems of their environment.

No amount of determination or industry can absolve flood victims from the almighty sin of innocence if they fail to try to understand and control their faulted land and its contrary waters. And so in the age of renewal the danger for the Church lies in the possibility that it may preoccupy itself with toilsome but twopenny tasks. The focus of concern can so easily be turned to the moment instead of the future, to accomplishing the incidental instead of confronting the real. Lippmann has caught some of this in his description of western men of consequence:

They have become . . . pragmatic, in the sense that they deal with the details of living and making a living and have put aside the great world. They do not have the ambition to participate in history and to shape the future. Modern men are predominantly isolationists. They are preoccupied with the more immediate things which may help or hurt them.

Some signs of renewal seem to be symptoms of this high order of isolationist innocence. Too many Christians of consequence have not really taken up the conciliar challenge to search the signs of the times. They have preferred an archeological aggiornamento that searches out the artifacts of the past. And this is to make the Church minister to museums rather than to the modern world. These maneuvers in the name of renewal reveal Catholics not as pilgrims to the future but as flood-routed victims bent on restoring their former way of life at the river's edge. They may speak of miracles but it is magic they invoke when they fail to look at the real issues and content themselves with the magnificent nonproblems of the 1960's.

These latter constitute an impressive category of concerns and they can be quickly reviewed by reading just the headlines of each week's issue of *The National Catholic Reporter*. These problems include celibacy, the liturgy, catechetics, the institutional Church, the creation of community within religious orders, and a dozen others. These are significant issues and I have addressed myself to several of them in this book. It is an attitude toward them, held by too many, that makes them nonproblems.

This nonproblem mentality fails to understand the lessons of history and distorts the issues of the day with an immature sense of values. Against the looming problems of the larger world these nonproblems can seem self-centered and self-satisfying. Catholics may sigh over them and even go so far as to solve some of them. The world might at that point make its own the words of the holy man, "And then what?" The world is not hanging breathlessly for the answers to our intramural difficulties. Men long ago settled most of these issues to their own satisfaction, and it is unlikely that they will change no matter what we decide. Many of these issues are so much a part of the past that they block the vision of what is really eating at man's innards in the present, and that is the future. The future has burst above the world like an errant rocket and its fiery motes fill the air around us. An age to come has inched in under our skin and infected us with a new and unnamed anxiety. This is no time for any Christian to be found with eyes only on himself or with his face set firmly in the general direction of the era of the "syllabus of errors."

Churchmen have stood in the slowly drifting confetti and watched too many parades going somewhere without them. They have sought restlessly to find a point of insertion that would make them genuine wayfarers with all of mankind. Impatient with failed approaches, they have tried everything from the offbeat to off-Broadway to reestablish their relevance to the world. But so many of these efforts have followed the other professions and arts rather than led them. In general, churchmen have found themselves imitating rather than inspiring the world. Little wonder they can put so much energy into their own problems. It is no surprise that theologians have begun to say that we are destined to be the remnant, widely scattered seeds in the resistant soil of civilization.

Peering into the past or at the nonproblems of the present prevents us from looking into the future which opens out as the greatest challenge but also the greatest opportunity for the Churches. Only when we see the world in the perspective of this onrushing age, do we face the real issues and discover the long-sought point of insertion into history. Anybody who can raise his eyes from his incidental concerns can see into the future. It is not all inky blackness and contingency. The forces that are shaping it are already identifiable in the present. The basic problem of the next generation will center on the meaning of man in the new environment he is creating for himself.

Man, born to be free, is heading into an age of extensive and subtle control of many aspects of his life. Some of these controls will follow his own choice, but many will be in the hands of his employers and governors. This is not to say that the elaborate mechanisms of observation and communication that will be every day realities will necessarily be misused. Nor can it be claimed that personal genetic control in choosing not only the number of one's heirs but also their sex, coloring, and even intelligence will be a bad thing. It will, however, represent a tightening of the environment, a subjection to subtleties of choice and persuasion that men have never known before. And here is man again, made, according to Christians, to labor, entering an age of incredibly expanded leisure. The great problem for the labor unions will not be managing man's hours at work but his hours away from it. Human beings, better schooled than ever in the advanced nations, will find their education may have prepared them for work that no longer needs doing or that is being accomplished by means other than men. Men, fully alive only when guarded by the Spirit, are entering a subsidized and sensate century. The forces that will forge these realities are already engaged, and no man can stay them. Men, if they are wise, can only prepare themselves for the new and unusual atmosphere of a postindustrial world.

The pressing problem will be the effect of these changes of scene on the principal actor and the hopeful hero of the drama of history, man himself. Brzezinski, a member of the United States State Department, catches the heart of the matter in these reflections:

In the second half of the twentieth century the developed nations, given new scientific and social developments, will face a real threat to the continued existence of man as a spontaneous, instinctive, rather autonomous and even somewhat mysterious being . . .

The real problem, and surely the most profound one for all religions, will be:

How will we preserve the integrity and freedom of man as an individual? As a physical being, he will become more malleable, given the trends of medical science. As a personality he will become increasingly subject to external manipulation, capable eventually of altering his behavior, his intelligence, his psychological state, his sexual state, in effect, himself. As man approaches the stage where he can "program" himself as he now programs his computer he may find himself increasingly denatured. The simultaneous weakening of religious belief may create both stress and emptiness . . .

What ails man, one observer has suggested, is the malady that can only be described as "future shock." With knowledge doubling every decade, with feats that even the most hopeful would have foresworn already achieved, men are already struggling, like logrollers in the rapids, to maintain their equilibrium. The projections of research organizations, such as the RAND Corporation and the Hudson Institute, suggest we are already involved in a basic transformation of our society. The interplay of automated industries and economic realities will work changes that will demand awesome adjustments in man's way of life.

Labor and leisure, the former already edgily and unsurely yielding its dominance to the latter, will exchange places in our economy and revolutionize it at the same time. With the guaranteed annual wage offering economic security and with the probability of massive leisure at his disposal, Western man will have to reconsider the Puritan ethic that led to prosperity, and its corollary that even pleasure must be work. Man will probably have a seven and one-half hour day, a four day week, ten legal holidays, and a thirteen week vacation every year. These arrangements already exist in some parts of the American world of work. Although there will always be those with the drive to do more, man will have to work only eleven hundred hours a year or forty per cent of his time. Leisure, piped to us as the basis of culture, will challenge his creativity.

But how indeed will this be managed? Our conviction that the greatest wisdom lies in governing ourselves will be challenged by even greater governmental intervention than at present in order to maintain some balance between the basic economic elements of supply and demand, creation and consumption. It is not beyond the realm of possibility that this incursion by others may also drastically affect child rearing and educational opportunities.

In the midst of these changes the extension of the life span and the possibilities of far longer periods of potential productivity for each individual will alter the familiar fundamental patterns of family life and career development. The urgent realities of supply and demand of talented people may limit the possibilities of a person's full participation in business, the arts, or government to a much smaller proportion of his increasing prime years. The age of retirement can only be lowered, and men may find a graduated two or three career life not only a possibility but a necessity. That husbands and wives will be physically capable of seeing one set of children into maturity and then starting all over again makes more than whimsy of Russell Baker's recent speculation about the "two-family family."

If these are genuine possibilities for the evolution of our present individual and social structures, they are also present for international society as well. The great gulf between the developed and the developing nations will increase. This may bring, as only one example, a polarization of racial tensions rather than a lessening of them. The white man's world will continue to outstrip the nonwhite man's world in almost every way. This continued disproportion of wealth and power between nations will only accentuate their differences and increase the tensions between and within them.

"If you do not think about the future," Galsworthy once wrote, "you cannot have one." Yet there is little evidence that men are preparing for the problems of this new world. We are still wed to modalities of thought which are simply neither flexible nor realistic enough to be vehicles of understanding or response to these developments. "Unlike the past," as Brzezinski observes, "when social change was slow enough to permit concomitant adjustments in man's outlook, today's pace of change is so fast that contemporary ideologies can hardly adapt to—even less anticipate—the problems of tomorrow. We are thus witnessing the spectacle of several major ideologies struggling to encompass the implications of

situations for which their systems made little or no allow-
ance." We tend to face radically different situations with ex-
pectations and beliefs left over from previous experiences.
We find comfort in translating the new in terms of the
familiar. This bridges the gap and blurs the startling reality
of the totally *other* quality of the innovation. So the loco-
motive was for us an "Iron Horse" although it spouted mechanical steam, not living breath. It was not a horse at all,
and a whole new set of categories of thought had gradually to
be accepted and absorbed to understand it as one of the signs
of the Industrial Revolution which refashioned society.

Man, in the face of planning for the future, tends, according to recent psychological studies, to lean toward the con-
servative course more often than not. The bias toward
choosing the more secure alternate prevents him from gaining the advantage of a timely decision in the other direction.
It is safer to wait and see than to risk all and possibly be
wrong. It seems that, more often than is profitable for man,
the risk is rejected. If this risk is later shown to have been
worthwhile (for example, to invest in IBM years ago at a low
price), man has forever lost the advantage of that decision.
Now he can only react to the new shape of reality (IBM at
over \$300 a share). Or he is forced now to do, to his disad-
vantage, what he could have freely chosen before. These
psychological defenses rob people and nations of the vision
to anticipate and plan adequately for their future.

Were an individual capable of recognizing and putting
aside these defenses, he could easily see the great hunger mankind will have for meaning in the world that is tumbling
toward us. In the balance of this century man will complete
the conquest and control of his external and internal environment. Then, at last, in his leisure, he will search out
more deeply the explanation and purpose of his existence.

Even now, we can hear the voices of men who have some glimpse of the future. Philosophers and theologians are struggling to develop modes of thinking about and speaking of God in an industrial society. But by the time their answers are formed, the boundary line into the post-industrial era will have been crossed. Dr. Timothy Leary presents psychedelic drugs as the sacraments of a new religion that will offer man a God within himself. At a half a cent a shot LSD and its companion drugs will seem to many to be the waters that wash them clean. Leary sees the new age as marked by a "resurrection of the body" in that man will find pharmaceutically-generated wonder within himself. Leary may be all wrong by many standards but he has the sense of the void of meaning to come and he believes that he has the medicine to fill it.

If, indeed, tomorrow's society will have even half of these characteristics, it will present the long sought point of insertion, "the door open and evident" to Christians who believe that they have the words of eternal life. Will the Churches be ready for the real problems of the survival of man and society in this new world? Can they make the hard decisions now that are needed for tomorrow without surrendering overmuch to the crippling counsels of caution to "wait and see" until the time for thoughtful planning is all used up? Our only hints are to be found in the sense of values that animates the present so-called renewal. The evidence is not encouraging.

Turned altars have not turned the tide for religion, and the liturgy in the vernacular seems still the song of an alien muse. Mildly altered rules in seminaries and vaguely promised opportunities for the layman hardly stand out as breakthroughs in the judgment of either friend or foe. No more fish on Friday has struck the bottom-most concern from the list of those things that could even be termed nonproblems. These hardly depict the Church with sure fingers on the pulse of humanity.

Renewal in religious life seems particularly fond of nonproblems. In a world waiting for those who can help it to learn the lessons of love and trust that will give it some chance of becoming a community, too many religious groups are concentrating on creating community only for themselves. Newly filled with personalistic awareness after a long siege of self-denial of even the most basic human relationships, many religious have made their own needs the pivot of what they would like to call progress. They are passing through an intermediate stage of development against the background of guitars and good time get-togethers. These phenomena are festive but foreshortened if they end at the enclosure. It is to the needs of men that we must respond and they are out there, already awash in the tides of a new epoch.

But why are these elements of renewal all too often superficial and innocuous? Do they not prevent us or protect us from a gritty confrontation with the genuine problems? And are they not signs that the future is already pouring into the present experience to bewilder all of us? Prelates and priests, the pious everywhere are face to face with the almost unbearable pressure of tomorrow and this is the source of universal unverbalized anxiety.

In a civilization that has battened by making obsolescence a source of economic growth, priests and religious are uneasy not only about their identity but also about their security in the calendar of the future. At the base, this is the gnawing, if unrecognized, fear of many candidates for the priesthood and religious life. At a primal reactive level of their being they are not sure that the lives they choose will be immune from this all-devouring obsolescence. It is little wonder that their theological heroes speak to them of an era of "religionless Christianity."

The younger clergy are sensitive to the voices of men who say, "We have seen the future and no one knows how it will work." It is a small wonder that in their groping they become impatient with elders who misunderstand them and mislabel their problems as those of authority and obedience, or belief versus unbelief. These categories are time-honored but also timeworn to a generation that is run out of the comforting kind of time that once allowed men to "make haste slowly." The seers who seed them with uncertainty and yearning are those like Whitehead who long ago wrote that:

The rate of change in our time is such that an individual human being of ordinary length of life will be called on to face novel situations which find no parallel in the past. The fixed person for the fixed duties, who in older societies was such a godsend, in the future will be a public danger.

We cannot reach the youth of today, whose environment of growth has been constant change and development, with the dreams and plans or even the realities of yesterday. The mythology of modern renewal resides in our delay over details that allow us to express our anxiety but which also distract us from its real source.

It is striking that one of the great themes of theological renewal and one of the great contemporary quotables, Teilhard de Chardin, both bid us to look deeply into our relationship to the future. Eschatology has been interpreted too often in terms of a last look at a world passing away. Visions of all of us gathered on some far frozen tundra as the aurora borealis of eternity lights up the sky have been the unwanted and unwitting fruit of some theological treatments of the subject. But the eschatological viewpoint rests on the foundations of living hope. It is a dynamic concept that demands an eternal openness to a world that is just coming to be.

In the same way, de Chardin has said that the Christian cannot live except in and for the future. His words must be more than poetic reveries about a Peter Pan "never never land". He did not write for dreamers and he did not write of happenings a thousand years hence. The lines of history, drawn long ago, are already converging. The dynamism of man's growth to the day when Christ will be "all in all" can only be activated by those strong and brave enough to be the real managers of hope for all mankind. Christians of today, liberated from the confines of the past, are the only ones who can deliver the much needed gift of hope for men in the future.

So many men have already given up in sorry and cynical celebration of "a world they never made." The arts have gone sour and dried up until they can only squirm and squeal the anguish of man on their multiplied stages. This is already an age when men feel that the odds are against them, that all the decks are stacked, and that their only exit is the one marked despair. The awesome gut problem of the present is to face the future in faith, to inform it with hope, and to give it the love that is man's sole source of life to the full. The world before us is indeed an apocalypse of all things made new. Only if we raise our heads toward it, can we place into proper perspective the concerns that consume us today. Modern day renewal needs to be demythologized so that we can get on with the real business of salvation history.

A healthy demythologizing will only occur when the great elements of Christianity are understood in their profoundly human setting. The liturgy is not intended to be artificial or archaic. When it is alive, it reflects and celebrates life itself.

It must flow out of the Christians who are truly attuned to their times. Right now the evident deadness of the liturgical renewal is related to the fact that it reflects a nonlife. It will be reinvigorated only when it pulses with the vital rhythms of men whose scars bear witness to their commitment to the human condition.

So too, theology must be a reflection on the Word Incarnate in our world. It cannot forever be backing and filling while the forces of history fossilize it even more. It must inform and illumine the great human issues of our time. It cannot treat man as if he were something stumbled upon by scholars on serendipitous journeys.

And the notion of community cannot stop short before the world of men. This is masturbation, not fruitful intercourse with mankind. The community must worship and praise God through its loving service to the world or the worship fails altogether. God still hates empty gestures or the blood of sacrifice splattered on his altars if these are divorced from a genuine and willing obedience to the needs of the human family. "In our era," Hammarskjöld once wrote, "the road to holiness necessarily passes through the world of action." The road through the future follows the same course.

The real evil in this world, Hannah Arendt has suggested, looks banal indeed. What a simple face it has. Ordinary men seemingly doing ordinary things, unaware of the extraordinary disasters to which their innocence contributes. Men doing decent and harmless things, as they see it, because they do not let themselves understand the cruel realities of their times. Evil does not bubble out of monsters onto an unsuspecting world. It grows in the void, in the emptiness men can so carelessly leave in life when they are unaware of what it is all about.

Religious who long for relevance must strip de Chardin's

words from their holy cards and jolly posters and plunge them into their own hearts. He can only be understood as an eschatological prophet, not as a multicolored folk hero. Otherwise our renewal will be self-defeating in its outcome. The trifles will triumph and the future, like so much of the past, will also be closed off from us. De Chardin felt the great rippling movement of the human race on its way to God. Only if we have the same feel of fundamental realities will we ever understand his words "Let us, then, for the love of our Creator and of the universe, throw ourselves into the crucible of the world of tomorrow."

11 / From Politics to Personalism

BEAUTIFUL theory always breeds practical problems. If we agree, even tentatively, that the institutions of the Church in the future will mold themselves on the model of healthy relationships, we must ask several pertinent questions. What exactly does this mean? How would it ever look in practice? How would people be prepared to live and serve the Church this way?

First of all, the use of the model of human relationships, especially that between man and woman, means that we must take Christianity seriously. No such model can be proposed unless we are committed to the values of human personality and the environment of faith, hope, and freedom in which the human person flourishes. There can be no compromise about trusting human nature. An end must be made to the age of words which fall on us like flood rains that wash away rather than nourish the land. The human persons who constitute the People of God must be treated as such in fact as well as in theory. They deserve freedom, respect, and responsibility in the apostolate. These are, after all, only the elementary conditions of life that any healthy person needs in order to give his or her wholeness to the Church. This concept reinforces the need to encourage and admit only healthy candidates into the priesthood or religious life. Only the healthy and mature can move into the free, cooperative life that the apostolate must be.

If we examine the notion of collegiality from a human point of view, it seems to demand that the apostolate, at all levels, be rooted in human relationships. We may talk of consultation and dialogue as though these were merely intellectual processes, but they imply a total personal relationship that reflects a real Christian sharing of life together. Collegiality demands that bishops and priests, priests and people live in a new and more open way with each other. This may indeed be difficult for the present generation of superiors or subjects to understand, because it runs so counter to the experience of their past lives.

The best hope for Christianity is that it become Christian through a collegiality that is incarnated in genuinely human fashion throughout the Church. This means, in effect, that the great basis for the future of the Church is Christians sharing life in open and trusting fashion even in the administration of the Church. This will be accomplished only with great patience. The future does not lie in the hands of dynamic charismatic leaders as much as it does in the whole People of God living and working together as a loving community. A corollary of this suggests that the truly effective leaders of the future Church will be men capable of collegiality. They must be men and women open to the Spirit in the interaction of sharing with their co-workers. This is the only way in which the true strength of the Church can be developed and expressed in a consistent and lasting way.

Following the basic principle of an incarnate collegiality, the structures of the Church will necessarily be smaller. They will emphasize individual growth and participation rather than detailed organization and group behavior. These smaller groups, whether they be of priests, religious, or lay people, or a combination of these, will exist always with a servant orientation toward the larger community of men in which they find themselves. The community of the future cannot exist for itself because it realizes that its growth and meaning will flow only from relationships to the people it serves.

The community of which we speak cannot, then, invest everything that is human in itself. It cannot hope to have relationships among its members which will be completely fulfilling or nourishing. It cannot feast on itself or it becomes a sign of sickness rather than salvation. That the members will be mutually understanding and supportive is undeniable but they must also be open and reach out to all the People of God around them. Relationships with others will be basically of service, but not in the sense that the community members go out to "do" something to others and then retreat to some "real" life within their own walls. Real life crumbles these walls. The service of others will be set in genuine human relationships that are not only an expression but also a legitimate source of growth. The community roots itself in, rather than makes apostolic forays on, the world of the People of God.

These future communities cannot exceed family size or they immediately begin to shift into the bureaucratic model of organization. The relationships of the members are the core of the community. The conditions of its existence must be such that these can develop in a healthy, if admittedly imperfect, human fashion. If collegiality is to be real, it can have its expression only in the personal sharing of the questions that arise in the course of life together. An orderly routine of meals and other functions may be necessary but cannot become the divinized model of community living. People do not gather together to keep rules but to share the same values and objectives, to be stronger together in the service of the Church than they possibly could be just as individuals. Plans and programs must be discussed openly. Granting that the superior's decisive power is preserved, he will be most effective when communication is quite open and personal. Orders of the day or anonymous directives relieve superiors of the personal challenge of collegial living; these methods of direction flourished in the era when communities grew cumbersome and impersonal. An apostolic community cashiers its commitment to human relationships when it resorts to these techniques. They flaw a community just as they would flaw a family.

The corollary of this, of course, is that the superior must indeed become the servant of the group. The position will no longer be sought because of its promise of power or its manipulative rewards. The superior is the person who must be open and sensitive to those with whom he or she shares life. Authority must be employed in these situations in a positive, constructive fashion rather than in a negative, controlling manner. The superior leads the community to greater growth and greater giving, but only if he can grow through giving himself to its members. This is no easy task, this becoming the servant of the servants. However, it does catch the New Testament concept of the meaning of authority. It creates the kind of communal environment in which the Christian ideal of authority as service rather than power can come into existence. This has been, almost necessarily, an unattainable ideal in the huge communities that have developed in the Church. The superior has, in these hulking corporationlike phenomena, been forced to coordinate and execute policy from the not so splendid isolation of

lonely power. He has had little choice but to feel guilty
because the conditions of bureaucracy have made the implementation of collegial personalism an impossibility.

One could easily speculate at this point about the psychological dynamics involved in shifting the emphasis within
the Church from authority as control to authority as service.
In a real sense, it requires the tempering of a masculine excess with healthy feminine elements. A mature balance of
these dimensions of humanity is required for the exercise of
authority in the renewed Church. This parallels the observations made by Tillich about the historical reorientation of
Protestant theology because of the impact of psychotherapy
and pastoral counseling:

One can say that psychotherapy has replaced the demanding yet
remote God by an emphasis on self-giving nearness. It is the
modification of the image of the threatening father—which was
so important in Freud's attack on religion—by elements of the
image of the embracing and supporting mother. If I were permitted to express a bold suggestion, I would say that psychotherapy and the experience of pastoral counseling have helped
to reintroduce the female element, so conspicuously lacking in
most Protestantism, into the idea of God.

Pastoral counseling and the research on psychotherapy
have highlighted the fact that an authoritarian, highly direc-
tive approach is not always constructive in helping individuals to achieve their fullness as persons. The authoritarian
position is convenient for the counselor or the leader whose
concerns are chiefly the implementation of his own viewpoint
and decisions. This can be highly effective when a strong
leader is dealing with an individual or group of individuals
who are willing to be led. This kind of relationship occurs
between a dynamic man and the masses who are convinced
that he has the right answer for their problems. Historically,

dictators have capitalized on this possibility to create highly effective, if often impermanent, totalitarian states. These leaders, charismatic beyond doubt, have not always promoted lasting growth in their followers. To do this would be to disturb the dynamic that enables them to have power in the first place. These leaders reinforce their own position by claiming godlike powers and infinite wisdom. In revolution-racked China, Mao and his words have necessarily been elevated to a metahuman status. Once the people begin to learn or to sense the meaning of personal freedom, such an authoritarian position is immediately questioned and challenged.

There is no doubt that the exercise of authority, even within the Church, has at times reflected these same tones of authoritarianism. For generations, for example, the faithful have been reminded of the superior training and wisdom of ecclesiastical authority. Censures, excommunications, and a whole armory of penalties have been used to maintain the elements of authoritarian structure. One of the aims of Vatican II was to redress the balance of the relationship between the bishops of the Church and the Bishop of Rome. Their authority, for example, is not something doled out to them from the total authority of the Holy Father. They possess it in their own right as successors of the Apostles to whom it was given directly by Christ.

It is understandable that the monarchical model of the Church, acquired through the cultural environment of the Church in time, emphasized many authoritarian practices. The difficulty lay, of course, in the eventual incompatibility of this model with the true destiny of the human persons who make up the People of God. The members of Christ's Body cannot be treated as a mass or as a mob that needs to be kept under control. Once the Church aligned itself irrevocably on the side of human freedom, authoritarian practices were doomed. This is not, however, to say that rightful authority was doomed at the same time.

Within religious life the monarchical model has also been reinforced by a number of so-called spiritual principles that served remarkably well for many generations. The self was to be despised and never trusted. Obedience was to be given unquestioningly to any order because, no matter how neurotic or illogical, this was "God's will." This blasphemy was probably one of history's most effective brain washing techniques. It has necessarily come into question in an era that has emphasized the dignity of each human person and his responsibility for his own life and decisions. A great grinding process of conflict is now under way as subjects shake off their willingness to forfeit human rights that in a truly Christian view of man can never be surrendered by anyone to anybody else. The People of God want to participate as full persons, not as children, in their Church. Many have observed that the crisis in the Church is indeed one of authority rather than obedience. This is an accurate description of the process of adjustment through which superiors are passing as authoritarianism expires as a viable ecclesiastical process. The desperate death throes of those who are wedded to authoritarian practice arises because they equate this with the true authority of the Church.

Curial-minded ecclesiastics have never been noted for trusting human beings or for hoping for much from mankind. They have preferred politics to personalism. People had to be controlled and formed, rather than freed and allowed to grow for themselves. This massive tangle of bureaucracy has had very little genuine sympathy with any democratic processes. These curialists have known no other way to administer the Church. It is no wonder that they resist so strongly the atmosphere of freedom and collegiality which are the soul of renewal. Their only response is to become more entrenched in their own positions, because they sincerely believe that this is the only way to save the Church.

But the Church, the person responding to the action of the Spirit, is struggling to find itself once more in the world of men. This person responds much as an individual in psychotherapy. The People of God need trust and freedom if they are to grow to their full maturity. A reflective and compassionate dimension is entering the Church to soften and balance the aggressive authoritarian positions of the past. In other words, the Church is seeking to discover and live truly the fullness of its internal experience. It is opening itself to the fact that there is more to the Church than masculinity. It is sensing its own feminine qualities and finding that they are not weakness but a different aspect of strength. Even as a mature man does not have to defend himself from his own gentleness by some form of denial or distortion, the Church is finding that its own fullness of personality is not frightening.

This process has only begun, however, and the Church's discovery of itself is not without moments of severe conflict and doubt. Authoritarianism will never be yielded by the Church's making some gigantic meditation resolution to do away with it. The delicate process of preserving and renewing the authority of the Church through healthy collegial relationships while putting aside the tactics of authoritarianism will occur in the same way that positive change does in an individual. The Church must change internally and this will continue to be an infinitely agonizing process. The stress of the present is the experience of this very growth. In the end, the Church will relinquish the authoritarian defense when its own inner sureness makes it unnecessary to be defensive anymore.

The Church will find new forms when it senses the fullness of its own masculine and feminine elements, when it can accept its true human composition through the realization that the Spirit reaches it only through the relationships of the persons who are the People of God. The Church will stand as a loving community whose life is service to all men when it fully understands and becomes itself. No longer will it stand in need of defenses because it will not be afraid of mankind anymore. It will stand in the open relationship that it is meant to have as an incarnate sign of redemptive love.

In summary, the great development of the Church as the People of God in this world demands a wholehearted embrace of its vocation of service. This includes a renewed understanding of the meaning of its authority and a rejection of authoritarianism in principle and in practice. This growth to a mature community of loving persons will depend on the Church's realistic acceptance of collegiality. This will develop only if the Church allows itself to experience the full measure of its balanced masculine and feminine elements. Otherwise authoritarianism will never yield to collegiality, and the last ditch struggle of those who have identified authoritarianism with authority will be prolonged and costly.

The forms of the future Church must be the setting for this growth and so they must never grow beyond the stage or size in which they can still be personal. The future of the People of God depends on the personal growth of each individual, and this is achieved, under the Spirit, only through their relationship with one another. The task of the individual in authority becomes, then, that of freeing rather than controlling the potential of community members. Exciting leaders cannot afford merely to have followers in the Church of the future. The really exciting leaders will not be those whose strength lies in being forceful individuals, but those whose strength is tempered with openness and willingness to share life with the subjects they thereby serve. This is not to rule out men or women of purpose and vision as vital to the Church of tomorrow. It is to emphasize that their leadership will not bring consistent growth unless they are capable of collegiality in the human condition. They must be capable of personal relationships that do not serve their own ends or needs. Their skills at human relationships cannot be those of a dictator or master salesman. Only through being genuine human beings who love others in a grown-up manner will these leaders open the People of God to the action of the Spirit. The forms for the future must all be designed to maximize the possibilities of sharing life in the Spirit by the People of God.

12 / Citadel or Community

I HAVE become increasingly aware of the widespread confusion that apparently exists for members of religious communities about the meaning of community itself. This is one of the most frequently asked questions at lectures and through the mails. These inquiries seem to be a symptom of uncertainty about the models that have come in the course of history to serve as the basis for religious life.

Many of the great saints who founded religious communities had clear convictions about the core of the shared life they proposed. Human relationships that were healthy, supportive, and productive of growth were foremost in their minds as they rallied their first members together. Joined to this was the presumed conviction that individual sanctification would arise in the context of the community's service to the needs of man. The Church can proudly point to the very real traditions and accomplishments of these groups that were so alive to Christian relationships in the world of men.

From a psychologist's point of view, which is admittedly not exhaustive, the meaning of community for these founders was expressed in intensely human ways. Religious communities were gatherings of people who were open to each other in sharing the purpose of ministering to God's people. They were groups of men and women who trusted and believed in each other. All these words arising from the same root seem to reflect this. Communion, communication: these are not theoretical or artificial life processes. They can be understood only in terms of the quality and depth of the personal relationships of the community members. Through these relationships, even as far back as the clustering of the Apostles at Pentecost (clearly with women present, according to the Scriptures, to share in their struggles), the Holy Spirit enlivened them for their servant vocation to the world. Wherever a healthy and productive community exists to this day, these realities of human relationships are the source of its energy and zeal.

This model has been obscured in the passage of history. An organizational model in which regulations rather than relationships became the binding and supposedly unifying force came into being. It is this distorted model rather than the ideal of communal sharing which has come into question in this day.

If religious communities are to survive in this new age, they must rediscover the vision and spirit of their founders and translate them into twentieth-century terms. This demands a sensitivity and a willingness to understand the lessons of history as well as the inexorable cultural factors which must be taken into account if communities are to be realities rather than revered relics in the future. One of the aspects of a founder's heritage that is often overlooked is his human relationships. The style or pattern of these in a founder's life frequently reveals much that is genuinely open and human. As has been mentioned, for example, there is a long list of founders or Church leaders who had deep and significant relationships with members of the opposite sex.

The history of many communities has followed a startlingly similar pattern. They were established to answer a need of the age. They constituted a response of faith to the crying problems of their times. In eras when civilization itself was unable or unwilling to provide these services, groups gathered to ransom captives, to nurse the sick, to care for the demented or the crippled, to provide shelter for orphans, or to establish schools with a Christian sense of values. Cultural conditions have, however, changed and, although the original purpose of their foundation may have been eclipsed, religious communties continued to find reasons for their existence. A subtle dynamic was involved in this. Communities, understandably enough, searched out reasons and works to keep themselves alive. Simply stated, they preserved at high cost their own existence even after their original purpose had already been accomplished. The ransoming of slaves is probably the most dramatic example of this.

We live in an age when it is no longer possible to do charitable works freely for those who need them. Modern day men are willing to pay through taxes and fees for the services that once had to be provided through charity. As a result, it is impossible to care for orphans, the mentally ill, the indigent, or the uneducated without the strong economic resources that are necessary to carry on these works. Noble as are their humanitarian callings, nurses, doctors, social workers, and teachers are affected by the economic realities. Strikes in these professions are now commonplace, and the lesson seems clear. One can no longer do anything for the needy unless he is able to compete financially for the professional services and facilities necessary for these works in the modern world. The handwriting in large letters is on the wall for communities which can no longer respond effec-

tively in a culture where their services are now being per-
formed by trained professional persons or agencies.

Caught in this difficult position, many of these communities have made survival their main thrust. Since they no
longer have their former relationship of altruistic service to
men, they concentrate on holding their community together
only for itself. To this end they have taken on new works
to keep themselves alive. A great many religious groups have
turned to works of education. Their effective presence in
this area of life has also recently been sharply questioned.
Many have taken on, with serious purpose, some missionary
activity on a relatively small scale. This has resulted in a
fantastic multiplication and reduplication of effort, with all
the diminished effectiveness this generates, within the
Church. This reality lay beneath the suggestions of the
Council document on religious life that such groups should
honestly reassess their effectiveness and even their continued
existence at this time.

Very few communities, of course, think that the Vatican II
Decree on Renewal and Adaptation is pointing to them.
Their present response to the crisis within the Church is
seldom an honest effort to find out whether they can feasibly
continue in existence. It is more often a regrouping of forces
or a reorganization aimed at preserving the life of the institute if this is at all possible. This is quite an understandable
response but all too often it leads the community to postures
which, in the long run, contribute to its ultimate collapse.

For example, a community may intensify recruitment
drives and be willing to compromise about the quality of
the candidates it accepts. This preserves the life of the community, but in a way that is clearly not healthy. The nu-
merical membership may remain constant but the deteriora-
tion of quality will eventually manifest itself. Second-rate

religious breed a succeeding generation of third-rate religious. Life at any cost simply does not justify this kind of maneuver in the name of community preservation. The individuals who are often accepted in these circumstances are the kinds of persons who can in no sense enter into the open and full relationships that are demanded by those who call themselves the community. They enter very often, as has been noted previously in these pages, for their own needs. They cannot, then, give themselves in service to the world around them, but for a while, in one of the saddest delusions of aggiornamento, they seem to keep a community in existence.

Communities which are experiencing the pressures of the modern age find themselves wedded to a definition of community which may not be flexible enough for the future. Their idea envisions a group of men or women who live in the same place and, with more or less general regularity, do similar work, perform the same religious exercises, and enjoy the same recreations together. This is a definition of community which depends heavily on physical presence and proximity. No sharing that depends on love can be so limited. A community need not live together in order to constitute a group of people who share a common purpose and support each other in it under the guidance of the Holy Spirit.

The insistence that all members of the community observe the same aspects of life has led to a number of painful situations. For example, communities find themselves divided between older members, who find adjustment to aggiornamento genuinely beyond them, and the younger members, who cannot change things fast enough. The superior usually finds herself between these factions in the thankless position of the peacemaker. She must care for the old and see that the young have the chance to grow.

Unfortunately, in too many convents or other houses of religion, there is the sacramentalized concept of trying to accommodate all these people through some concessions to each in the matter of community life. This arises from the unquestioned conviction that community life means that everybody must do the same thing in pretty much the same way. Untold misery and suffering have arisen because people have been unwilling to look for alternate solutions to this difficulty. It is simply not true that a community must find its members sharing exactly the same kind of life at all levels. Huge communities, even when their movements are regulated like those of the Rockettes, have not really accomplished anything by preserving this framework of common life. This is all too often empty and unsatisfying for many members of the community.

Far more realistic, in this time of change, is to break down these communities into subgroups or subcommunities which enable the development of compatible and healthy relationships and which are allowed to function with a good deal of autonomy. The mass community model must be broken soon in any case. A good starting point would be to divide communities according to the interests and preferences of the members. The older sisters or brothers, for example, should not be expected to take on new prayer lives which are unappealing and unsatisfying for them. They can be allowed to have a life that is very much their own and which allows them to spend the last of their days as they have always spent them. The younger members can constitute groups of their own. They will no longer feel guilty for being young and interested in change. Neither will they be subjected to the incredible tensions that are present in communities where large segments of new breeders and old breeders are pitted against one another.

This is a startlingly obvious solution but it is one that has been largely overlooked. To subdivide takes a little creativity and ingenuity but it is not an impossible task. These communities must be so treated, or there is very little probability of their survival in the future. The new generation of vocational prospects will simply reject the option of leading a life that dries them up and cuts them off personally, spiritually, and socially from their fellow members in the total community of Christ.

The forms for the future will necessarily embrace new forms of community that are not so dependent on one schedule and one way of doing things. It is not unusual for individuals to realize that, although they may live many miles apart and may see each other only infrequently, something about their deep relationships with each other makes them a real community. The genuine communities in the world are made up of people of common purpose who have shared in the same struggles and who will open themselves in this sharing to the action of the Spirit. Their community is not one of physical presence but the kind that only arises in life that is shared in the Spirit. The false god of physical community must give way to new forms that will be more mobile and that will not be circumscribed by the parameters of time and space.

The communities that will count in the future will arise between people who understand each other and whose presence, even at a distance, makes a profound difference in each other's lives. This is the kind of concept that Andrew Greeley developed in his illuminating essay on the "new community." A concept like this fits into the sociological realities of tomorrow. Because this more nearly defines the meaning of community many religious communities are already revealed as artificial and pain-filled entities. They are not inhabited by people who are enjoying human relationships with each other as much as by people who are going through the same motions, all too often ritualistic, together.

The openness to sharing life together under the inspiration of the Holy Spirit must precede and serve as the basis for any gathering of community members. It is this quality of genuine love and understanding which holds people in communion despite the barriers of time and distance which seem to threaten it. People who love and share a common purpose of giving themselves for the sake of God's people constitute the real communities in this world. People must have experienced some mature human sharing before they gather together in communities. That is, in fact, the reason people gather together into physical communities. All too often it has been presumed that the physical community itself would create the conditions of sharing that are the signs of real community.

The communities of the future, then, cannot follow any highly restrictive mold. Their planners must be open to the kinds of forms that will best express the genuine underlying human relationships which make them realities that are signs of God's loving presence in the world. The communities of the future may live together or they may come together only at times. This coming together, whenever it occurs, should center on the celebration of the Liturgy. It is in the sharing of the Eucharist that members of a community find their deepest moments of identity in Christ himself. It is through opening themselves to each other in the heart of the mystery of Christ's own sacrifice that community members realistically find themselves and return with a surer gift of themselves for other men.

This raises pertinent questions about the celebration of the Liturgy. It must indeed reflect the life and struggles of the members who are serving, perhaps in a variety of ways, to make God's presence and peace felt in the world. Community members must bring some maturity to the Liturgy, or it will become a plaything in which they will act out their adolescent needs rather than discover the richness of their manhood and womanhood. People who are alive bring vitality to the Liturgy. The Liturgy is not magic and it is not just a good show. It is the great occasion for people who face the truths about themselves and life itself to celebrate the separation of Christ's Body and Blood which is so magnificently and paradoxically the source of their unity.

Values like these transcend many of the notions that have developed over the years and that have presented a pale imitation of Christian life as the ideal of community observance. For example, "loyalty" to the community has dictated that people do not talk about faults of others, that they deny realistic difficulties out of some sense of foreign-legion friendship for one another. This is far different from faith in a community. The latter is far more demanding because it demands that we invest ourselves in others, that we open ourselves in a real sharing of what we are with one another. All this is done, not to protect each other's reputations, but for the sake of the People of God. This is the justifying cause of bringing communities together in the first place. They cannot exist for themselves and they cannot in our culture or in any other culture desperately look about for the means that will preserve their life even when history has already closed its books on their presence in the world of men.

Another false sense of loyalty is that which suggests that the members avoid the tensions of dialogue and leave all the burden for the community's growth on the superior. This is to short-change a community, out of some exaggerated and not necessarily Christian sense of duty. This attitude breeds the "peace at any price" compromises that so often characterize weak communities that are afraid of conflict, they do not realize that conflict can be creative. Collegiality does not rule out the mature exchange of attitudes and opinions. This is, in fact, essential to effective collegiality.

In the same vein, one of the great pseudo virtues of community observance has been something called "charitableness." This means to refrain from the petty crimes of talking about one's neighbor and to indulge in fancies that enable us to put always a good interpretation on somebody else's behavior. This is a way of withdrawing from reality altogether under the guise of Christian love. There must be something better in life than this for people who wish to give themselves to Christ and his suffering members. This idle game of seeing, thinking, and speaking no evil has been proposed as one of the models of how a good religious lives his life. These are the days in which people hunger for what is real. They will literally not swallow offerings that are such insubstantial imitations of life itself.

Charitableness, as a hypocritical, Victorian practice, bears no relationship to the kind of love that frees men's spirits and brings them to life again. This is the only kind of love that will allow communities to survive in the future. It is the action of the Spirit that works through human relationships in its effort to transform the face of the earth. The forms for the future must make room for the fierce fire that is the presence of the Spirit. All that is imitation, all that is artificial and archaic, all that is done in compromise to preserve forms from which life has genuinely fled, will pass away. The Church will depend on the full life of those who are joined through the Spirit in giving themselves totally to the service of the People of God.

It seems clear that if community is to be a more flexible concept in the future, the lives of those who serve the Church will also have other characteristics as well. The first of these will be greater freedom and independence. A priest and the religious man or woman will live a responsible life that is not linked nearly so much to a territorial place or set of practices as has been true in the past. The value of the servant of the Church in the future will lie in the quality of his or her life. He or she is called primarily to serve the people rather than an institution, and the great condition for this will be much more independence of life. Convent and rectory life as we know them will be modified considerably, and although there will be great difficulties involved in working these things out, this independence of existence within the larger community will be a reality within a very short period of time.

All the signs of the present times point in this direction. The experiments with extra-territorial parishes, the seeking for points of insertion within the professions, the obvious need for life in the world if one is going to affect the world positively—all these substantiate what was underscored so sharply by the Vatican II documents which emphasized freedom as an essential condition of human life. It is also important to allow genuine freedom of private life for community members. They must be free to relate with individuals and groups outside their own community.

It is inconceivable that the Church could endorse freedom for all mankind and not come to insist upon for its own servants at the same time. This is absolutely necessary for any effective service to the community of men in the future. This is why it is necessary to be flexible about the ideal of community living and to explore the many manifestations this can have in people who are open to the Spirit of Love.

One of the undoubted models for a future community of this type will be the apostolic team which will be small enough to constitute a viable community and which will reflect, at the same time, all of the elements that constitute the Church as the People of God. The success of these teams will demand the qualities of openness and maturity that will also serve as a model for the rest of the Christian community. These teams, and examples of them already exist in the world, will be composed of priests, religious, both men and women, and lay people who will pool their efforts to bring the good news of salvation not just to a parish or a school or some interested organization. It is quite possible that such teams can operate within the arts, secular education, government, and any of the other of the activities that are part of the life of the family of man. These teams will necessarily respond to culture as it presents itself rather than demand that culture reshape itself to make room for some antique form of community which no longer has any significance.

We have been humbled in our efforts to look into the future only by the impoverishment of our own imaginations. We have been cautious because we have been afraid of all the things that man can do wrong. We have felt that he must be controlled and guarded or his choices will lead him always down the wrong paths. That kind of caution has brought us to the present state in which we are finally realizing that we must draw in our breath and take that tremendous risk of coming alive in the real world. We must depend on human relationships as the rich source of our inspiration by the Spirit. It is necessary to open ourselves personally and depend on that, rather than on all the dreadful impersonalities that we have let obstruct the Spirit over the years. The fundamental virtues of faith, hope, and love must prevail if we are to have a future at all.

We have sketched only a few of the general characteristics of forms that will fit men better and enable them to express their full humanity in relationship to mankind. It is for those who are creative and bold, for those generous enough to affirm their commitment to the Spirit who leads them on to give themselves even unto death, to chart the further course of salvation history. Forms will vary but they will have the fundamental characteristics we have described in this chapter. The forms for the future, like the altar of old, will be for man, not man for the forms. It is through these forms which capture and express man that the Holy Spirit will re-create the face of the earth.

13/Training for Tomorrow

I LIVE in a symbolic seminary, not so much because of what goes on inside it but because of what has happened outside it. For years it stood, a transplanted piece of New England brick and bell tower architecture, on a ridge that runs like a wrinkle through the Illinois flatland. The great city lay east. Those who looked could see a pulsing red glow playing against the night sky, the vigil lights of the secular sacramental presence of Chicago. Miles of farmland, rich and black almost beyond belief, surrounded and soothed us.

But the city has long since burst its dikelike boundaries and rivered out onto the land, not uprooting houses but planting them by the thousands. Just awakening, as most seminaries have, to the fact that we must reach out to the city of man, we have discovered that it had no time to wait, that it had in fact reached out and embraced us. Every training house finds itself in the same position. The psychological and theological center of gravity for the Church has shifted radically and the seminaries, caught off balance, have had to struggle to establish a new equilibrium.

There were many early signs, particularly in Europe, of ferment in the seminary world. Experiments in training for and living the apostolate were noted with interest but stimulated little action elsewhere. Right up until the Second Vatican Council, most American seminaries maintained their state of original innocence. Suddenly, or so it seemed, the well-ordered serenity of these institutions dissolved, and rebellion rather than recollection became the disorder of the day. Unheard of protests occurred as the new breed filled their lungs with the fresh air of freedom that began to blow like a gale through the windows opened so gingerly by Pope John.

Some seminaries reacted as men often do in the face of news so threatening that they cannot absorb it. "No, it can't be," men utter when, for example, they hear news of a shocking and unexpected event, such as the assassination of President Kennedy. When psychologically assaulting, the new is fended off by outright denial of it. In the normal person, however, there is a gradual but accurate admission of the truth of the event to their consciousness. This is followed by a necessary and again altogether normal period of mourning, during which the individual readjusts his whole being to a new order of things. Mourning ends when this is complete and the person, with a new understanding of himself, can enter into the flow of life once more. Difficult and wrenching as the task is, the dead have to be buried so that the living can carry on.

Most seminaries are just laying the past to rest and are struggling to reidentify themselves in a living relationship to the new face of the Catholic world. Others, however, have not got beyond the stage of denying the news that the formerly vigorous model of seminary training died suddenly and intestate in the early 1960's. In some areas of Catholic life this mechanism of denial has extended to the entire experience of Vatican II. But, just as the person who denies death and does not allow himself to mourn develops internal and unsettling conflicts, so the seminaries which have failed to face the new realities are also suffering from self-inflicted and self-defeating uncertainties.

Renewal in the world of seminary and religious training has proceeded at an uneven pace because of the mixed reactions to postconciliar realities. But the age of monastic removal from the world has indeed ended. The past must be mourned appropriately so that a readjusted and effective life can begin. It is the genius of Americans to be flexible in matters like these. As far back as 1883 the bishops who were preparing the agenda for the Third Plenary Council of Baltimore rejected the proposal of summer villas for seminarians. They did not want American priests trained in seclusion from the world in which they would serve. Bishop McQuaid eschewed the "time-consecrated miseries and needless sufferings" of other institutions of priestly formation. "There is no justifiable reason," he wrote, "why Church authorities in America should be hampered by the customs and usages of older countries, where innovations are looked on in the light of sacrilege."

If this same kind of vision is to prevail in the period of adjustment through which we are passing, it must be marked with a similar strong sense of reality. The task for the seminary educators of America, through the National Episcopal Conference, is to develop a program of apostolic education and personal formation which meets the needs of the times.

The former seminary system, and the same holds for the preparation of religious and laymen for the apostolate, was carefully thought out and achieved its purposes quite well. A particular form of life was presented to candidates and this was to serve as the stable framework for their years in the service of the Church. It based itself, in most aspects, on the monastic ideal.

This did not conflict with the conditions of priestly and religious life as they existed well into the twentieth century. The priest, for example, was trained to meditate before Mass, to recite his breviary, to do his spiritual reading, and to perform other acts of personal devotion which were quite compatible with the demands on his time and service. Until the Decree on Frequent Communion, issued by St. Pius X, Catholic life provided a certain amount of leisure in which the young cleric could carry over his seminary schedule into his life in the priesthood. The altars that can still be found in the sacristies of older country churches attest to the fact that the priest did not say Mass every day for his people because daily Mass attendance was not a commonplace of Catholic life. Confessions were not the steady burden in this age in which the priest had not yet become deeply involved in a wide range of activities of service to his people.

The twentieth century saw an evolution in the demands made on the schedule of the apostolic priest. He became involved in teaching, in social and youth work, in an unrelenting schedule of marital and personal counseling. In short, the priest's life was changing radically even as the country itself was shifting from a predominantly rural to an urban form of living. The conflict arose because, although the life of the priest was being modified, the seminary system was not. In the main, it still equipped the priest with the model of a dedicated and slower-paced life while culture was robbing him of the leisure in which to lead it. In various ways priests made their own personal adjustments to the service-oriented apostolate. They often felt uneasy, however, because they could no longer live the model of the spiritual life proposed to them in the seminary.

These issues have been at the heart of renewing seminary training. A man cannot be successfully prepared to lead a life of the Spirit in a hurried and unforgiving world by training adapted from a monastic ideal of existence. The present period of adjustment is marked by too little comprehension of this fact. It is not enough merely to change the seminary schedule so that there is more free time and less supervision from authorities. It is not only ineffective but disastrous to break down the seminary walls unless one has a sure sense of what form of life is to be introduced after they crumble.

Most conscientious seminary men understand the general dimensions of the challenge. Under great pressures they are attempting to improve the realism and the quality of seminary education. At present they are trying to shift the emphasis from forming a man from the outside to the creation of environments in which he can truly develop from inside himself. A transition from obedience to prudence as the core of seminary life is under way. This is not a worldly prudence but the healthy prudence which St. Thomas saw as the central and coordinating virtue of Christian life. It can be said that in the seminaries where the issues of the day are being met, there is a genuine effort to develop structures that match the nature of man and the realistic demands of the priestly and religious life. This is the kind of renewal based on truth, not just on a reaction to the past.

The next phase of seminary renewal must go even further if it is to concretize the possibilities that have been envisioned by the theology of the Church in the documents of Vatican II. An understanding of what the new seminary should be will flow only from a deep commitment to what the Church already is. The Church has presented itself as the mystery of the People of God. This deeply human definition must be kept in focus in the development of training houses intended to prepare servants for the Church. The highly bureaucratic concepts of the Church as some organizational monolith must be put aside. It is not an ethereal General Motors in which the hierarchy is the management and principal stockholder, the laypeople are the hired hands, and from which sacramental graces come like dividends. The Church is a people, human beings in relationship to one another, men and women breathed on and guided by the Spirit as they make their way through history. It is God's People struggling to live in his Presence and to give themselves to his work in the world.

The Church is, then, a mystery of human relationships and it cannot be understood at all except in these terms. If the seminaries are to produce priests who can truly minister to the needs of these people, they must imbue themselves with a sense of the true nature of the Church. This can only be accomplished if we are willing to end our mourning period for the past. We must also put aside uncomfortable compromises with the present and think in radical terms about the seminary of the future.

An entering seminarian or candidate for the religious life should begin to live in the Church from his very first moments of preparation. The training house must constitute itself as an experience of the Church itself. It must reflect and express this mystery of the People of God and introduce its students into their servant vocation in a realistic way. Obviously, the seminary must maintain high educational standards but, as a school, it must be set in a vital experience of the redemptive mission of the Church in action. The seminary cannot afford merely to theorize about the Church, to talk about something that the students will encounter at a later date. In every way that is reasonable and sensible the seminary should *be* the Church in its particular locality.

Several points are connected with this. The great problem faced by seminaries has been to provide apostolic experience for its students. These activities have proliferated in the present day but they have seldom been carefully planned or professionally supervised activities. Apostolic activities have had, in many situations, a distinctly adolescent flavor. They have been occasions for the students to get away from the seminary, to visit the inner city, the jails, or even foreign lands in search of God's People. Curious corollary behavior has also developed with these moves. Since there are few seminary professors who possess either the skills or the time to supervise and confront the seminarians with their real responsibilities in these activities, the experiences have had a generally random character. The student might learn something but the chance that it would be a consistent and constructive process has been small.

Seminarians and religious candidates, full of youthful generosity, have embraced these apostolic ventures wholeheartedly. It is not altogether their fault that they have satisfied their own needs through them to a much larger degree than was good for them or the people with whom they worked. To create the situation in which seminarians use the people they are supposed to serve is a dreadful repetition of one of the worst features of clerical life. Quite quickly, however, a major problem in this regard has developed in many seminary programs of apostolic work. The seminarians find that they enjoy the hospitality of families outside the seminary walls. They can contrive elaborate and all too often self-serving expeditions into the world of men. The enjoyment of the individual has often enough become a major attraction of this newly developed feature of seminary life.

All too often the opportunities that have been created to enable seminarians and young sisters to work together in apostolic ventures have turned into adventures in "relating" that bear little resemblance to mature behavior. Much of this occurs because the activities have been poorly supervised. Supervision does not mean chaperoning. It means that apostolic work should have supervision comparable to that in medicine, law, and psychology. Seminaries have largely failed to deal with the fundamental question of what it means to be responsible for other persons.

This question of being responsible for another is probably the most maturing experience that any human being can have. It is one of the gut confrontations of life itself, and for too long seminary education has failed adequately to come to grips with it. Being responsible for the person of another is fundamental for anybody who proposes to give his life in love for others. It is the experience that a husband must have in relationship to his wife. It is what parents must have in relationship to their children. It is a uniquely demanding experience because it is compounded of the rich elements of faith and trust and real concern. If these are to be the hallmarks of any pastoral relationship, then the seminarian or religious candidate must begin to understand and experience them as early as possible.

Too frequently priests have exhibited a lack of feeling for this dimension of personal responsibility. They could be involved in the lives of others but were always able to keep the degree of their self-investment under their own control. They could visit and dine with families and get a refreshing experience for themselves. But they could always go home when the dishes had to be done or the children had to be put to bed. The sustained experience of all that responsible family living entails was not a part of their lives. It is little wonder that so many could idealize marriage with no sense of the aching demands on each other that even people who deeply love each other experience.

A classic example on the seminary level is the student who, during his holidays, would strike up an acquaintance with a young girl but never reveal to her that he was a seminarian. He always held that in reserve, a safeguard that permitted him to enjoy the relationship without ever really giving himself seriously to it. The summer would draw to an end and he could pull out to return to what he felt was his noble calling. Unrecognized and unappreciated by him would be the effects of his behavior on the girl in question. He was, however, responsible for her and her welfare but never confronted himself enough to realize it. This quality of being in and out of people's lives, of never opening themselves to the fact that they cannot simply toy with or use people, has already characterized the lives of many priests and religious.

Seminaries have not distinguished themselves in making their students face themselves in the context of responsible relationships with other persons. Without malice, surely, they have enabled seminarians to play at life more than enter into it as deeply as possible. The great empty yearning to be "where the action is" is no substitute for placing oneself quite openly into the world "where life is lived."

If the Church is servant rather than master, this central theme of responsible service to God's People must pervade every training house that hopes to survive into tomorrow. When I speak of fashioning the seminary into an experience of the Church for those who enter it, I place this quality of taking on the obligations of a man in relationship to other men as the most important of all. Without an insight into this dimension of human living, the seminary cannot in any acceptable way express itself as the servant Church.

To constitute the seminary as an incarnation of the Church in a particular place is to emphasize its immediate relationship to its environment. It must serve the community and people in which it finds itself. Too many seminaries are still rather mysterious places even to the Catholics who live nearby. If this seminary is more than a building, just as the Church is more than an institution, then it cannot relate to anything but the concrete situation in which it finds itself. The seminarian or religious candidate must step into a training house that senses its relationship to the needs of its community and gives itself generously in response to these. To make this a reality, it is suggested that each seminary, not only as divided into small groups, but also as a real total Christian community, take on some pastoral responsibility in its area. There may be great difficulties in establishing even relatively small parishes in connection with seminaries, but these are insignificant in the light of the positive gains that can thereby be achieved.

In other words, the seminary must become a local Church in the sense that it reflects the Church's awareness of its commitment to the world around it. It must consciously be a sign of what it teaches about or it fails to re-create the mystery of God's Presence. This does not mean that all the faculty members must at the same time be parish priests, but some, at least, must live out the pastoral role in the context of the seminary. The apostolic activities of the seminarians will be ordered to the pastoral character of the seminary as servant to its environment. The seminarians must interact responsibly with the people who are at the very doorstep of the seminary. Only in this immediate and demanding setting will the faculty members ever be able to supervise the seminarians' apostolic works in a way that will promote their growth as genuine servants of the People of God. The great awareness that must pervade the seminary is its obligation to respond to its surrounding community in genuinely Christian fashion. It can no longer hide away in the hills. The seminary of the future must relate itself to flesh-and-blood men or it provides a framework that only talks about the People of God but never really shares life with them.

Just as the seminary must be rooted in a servant relationship that is vital and maturely responsible, so too it must reflect the nature of the Church in other ways. The faculty, for example, should not be composed only of priests. If this is so, the seminarian experiences merely the clerical Church, and this is not to experience the total Church at all. The faculty should consist of men and women, religious and lay persons, as well as priests, if it is to contribute to the seminarian's experiencing of the Church during his years of formation. In line with this, the professional responsibilities of the priest will no doubt diminish as the years go by. First of all, there will not be enough priests to staff seminaries in the handsome manner of a former age. Secondly, the priest will more appropriately live out his pastoral vocation if he can be freed from the responsibilities of teaching. More and more, the role for the priest in seminary training will be that which allows him to live fully within the seminary the role he has in the Church.

The seminary itself, as a dynamic expression of the Church, will also begin to understand its function within the diocese more clearly. In many ways it can be the key to renewal. The seminary possesses the resources and the facilities, especially with the addition of pastoral responsibility, to become the great source of apostolic formation and experimentation in any diocese. It can provide the conditions for healthy experimentation in pastoral approaches and liturgical development. The seminary can easily become the center for the continuing education of the clergy and religious of the area.

The seminary must become something more than a modified monastery. It should serve as the source of apostolic energy and development in every diocese. These possibilities have been largely overlooked but they represent the only healthy direction which training for the priesthood and religious life can take. These aims are perfectly consonant with the theology of Vatican II and the crying needs of the Church at this time in history. Only our impoverished imaginations prevent us from seeing the radically new and effective sign of salvation that seminaries must be in the new Church.

Practical considerations also point to the fact that we need fewer seminaries as well as much greater collaboration and sharing of facilities on the part of healthy workers in the area of religious and apostolic formation. No one seminary in any archdiocese can move into the future unless it develops more cooperative relationships with the other houses of training in the same jurisdiction. Unless this occurs we will have a continued proliferation of relatively weak and ineffective programs.

It is probably true that the seminary of the future will open itself logically to candidates other than seminarians. This is so, first of all, because the basic religious and theological formation for all workers in the apostolate will become more similar in the years ahead. This kind of quality education cannot be reproduced in every house of formation in a diocese. A central house of training for all those who will give themselves to the service of the Church in a particular diocese will become a necessity. This will break down many of the unfortunate barriers that have existed between religious and secular priests and will also offer the opportunity for healthy and mature relationships between the men and women who want to give themselves to the Church.

There is no way in which the richness of the relationships between the Church's men and women can be successfully developed unless there is a great deal more sensible preparation for it during the years of training than there is at present. The task begins with the adult men and women of the Church. They must forge the cooperative relationships that extend down into the years of training or something very different and very unhelpful will occur. The young seminarians and sisters, groping for ill-perceived personal values, will seek out relationships on their own level, and the result can only be confusion. If the Church is men and women, then it has to be that way during periods of preparation for the apostolate as well. There is no good reason why several training houses cannot be established in close relationship with a central seminary. These can be the residences for sisters, brothers, and laypeople. It is never too early to face them with learning to work and relate together in a healthy and open way. This is one of the areas where the dimension of what it means to be responsible for another person must be strongly and realistically underscored.

Some will say at this point that there is a great danger that some of these candidates will fall in love and get married. That is true. It is a risk well worth running. The others will make a much better informed response to the gift of celibacy.

The great task of helping the Church to realize its fullness through the relationships of its men and women must be approached in this new age with something other than the indirection and mistrust of former times. It is the contention of this book that if the Spirit works through human relationships, it will reach the human community in the richest way through the relationship of man and woman. Men and women within the church open each other to the action of the Spirit whenever they have a deeply mature and respectful relationship with one another. There is, in my opinion, no substitute for this in the development of the human persons who would become apostles.

The whole question has been treated with a very narrow vision of the meaning of celibacy and chastity. Everything has been done to preserve the men and women of the Church in worlds quite separate from one another. Romanticism, sentimentality, fear, and a wide range of other uneasy reactions have characterized the traditional preparation of young men and women for their lives in the Church. I submit that most of these approaches have not only been inhuman but unsuccessful. I have tried to review some of the dimensions of our failure to face the rich possibilities of a more human understanding of the vowed men and women in the Church and their relationships with each other and with the rest of the People of God.

Recently there has been a great stirring of interest in the healthy possibilities of a better human base for the relationships of the men and women who are the servants of the Church. The time has come to provide the models and principles of mature cooperation between the sexes within the Church. The seminary or training house of the future is crucial in this regard. Unless the adults within the Church provide the conditions of life and the set of Christian values indispensable to genuinely holy celibate dedication, there will be serious misunderstandings and mistakes on the part of those who are not yet adult. The great opportunity for the gradual development of structures that will express dedicated celibate lives as signs of generous love will also be missed. The People of God will be the poorer for this.

Men and women who are already fully grown must begin to work together to fashion the training house as a living reflection of the Church. They must meet in adult situations, not to defend themselves from each other, but to open up the possibilities of greater work together for the sake of the whole Church. They must interact on educational boards, in commissions for the renewal of seminaries and religious life, in the heart of the apostolate itself, or one of the richest opportunities for the growth of the Church will be lost.

The growing understanding of the nature of man, the temper of the times, and the needs of God's People—all of these demand a response that is positive and constructive at this point in salvation history. Although this is a difficult as well as a delicate challenge, it is also one that cannot be ignored. Neither can the response to it consist of the elements of fear and flight that have been so much a part of our tortured past. The great efforts at improving seminaries and houses of training as authentic models of the Church itself provide the logical and sensible setting for dealing intelligently with the relationships of the Church's men and women. The world will simply not be saved by men and women separately. The time for forging healthy apostolic forms of training and service is now.

The Church can never speak relevantly to men unless it presents itself in the fullness of its human character. Nobody will listen to men and women who can only theorize or sing about love in a self-saving manner. The Church is called to express the action of the Spirit through its human members to the whole human family. The men and women who serve the People of God must face themselves, not as individuals with some idea that their dedication is a choice not to love, but as fully grown persons who realize that their commitment is a positive choice to love. There is no substitute for real love in the apostolate. In the same fashion, there is no substitute for what only the house of apostolic formation can do to ready men and women for lives that must be essentially gifts of themselves in love to others.

It is precisely because love is more than poetry and Bible quoting that the training programs of the future must reach into the innards of the next generation of priests and religious. A veneer of seemingly pious practice is not enough in a world long grown weary of loveless religions. We must demand that the fullest possible manhood and womanhood be realized in candidates for the service of the Church. That is why it is so essential to ground the training for tomorrow in life-situations that do not hint at but demand responsible personal behavior. Individuals must grow into the service of the Church through serving others with a deep consciousness of their responsibility for other human beings. Without this as the foremost dimension of training, pastoral care can never be an effective expression of Christian love.

In summary, the training for tomorrow must have its roots in the reality of today. A sense of what life is really about, the demands of genuinely trusting and caring for others— these are the core elements in the formational program. Houses of training must offer an experience of life in the Church itself. The servants of the Church for tomorrow begin to serve responsibly through involvement in the local servant Church that the training house must become. All the true elements of the People of God must participate in this experience, or there is a seriously faulted representation of

the Church. The training house of the future must open itself to both the men and women of the Church so that they
can begin to share the burdens and obligations of the apostolate together as effectively as possible. Healthy relationships
must be developed during the years of training, or the great
possibilities of service together for the sake of the People
of God will not be realized.

In the end we depend totally on the Spirit. Our task is to
prepare ourselves as wholeheartedly as possible for his action. Forms for the future can only try to make our humanity
as available as possible for his inspirations. The Spirit reaches
us in our human relationships, in the great opening of ourselves that only occurs in the context of our response to each
other as human beings. All our effectiveness as loving mediators in the world of men springs from this.

Near the end of the play "Philadelphia, Here I Come"
there occurs a scene in which the young hero's inner voice
speaks a challenge to the parish priest. The Canon, oblivious
to the desperate yearnings of both father and son to reach
each other with a few words of understanding and love before the son leaves for America, contentedly plays checkers.
He is a sign all right, a sign of insensitivity in the midst of
the family struggling for some small sharing before the
night ends. The inner voice cries out to him ". . . you could
translate all this loneliness, this groping, this dreadful bloody
buffoonery into Christian terms that will make life bearable
to us all . . . Why, arid Canon? Isn't this your job, to translate? Why don't you speak then?"

It might as well be the anguished voice of all humanity
addressed to all of us who are meant to be translators of all
that is painful into something bearable and meaningful.
Only if we are deeply human and keenly sensitive to the

needs of the human family can we live fully our servant role as mediators, as translators of life into Christian terms. ". . . Why, arid Canon? Isn't this your job, to translate? Why don't you speak then?"